FILM FLUBS
The Sequel

Even More Memorable Movie Mistakes

FILM FLUBS

The Sequel

by Bill Givens

A Citadel Press Book
Published by Carol Publishing Group

10 9 8 7 6 5 4 3 2 1

Film Flubs™, Son of Film Flubs™, and Film Flubs, the Sequel™ are registered trademarks of Bill Givens.

Library of Congress Cataloging-in-Publication Data

Givens, Bill (Bill H.)
  Film flubs, the sequel : even more memorable movie mistakes / by Bill Givens.
   p. cm.
  "A Citadel Press Book." ISBN 0-8065-1360-8
  1. Motion pictures—humor. 2. Motion pictures—Miscellanea. I. Title.
  PN1994.9.G588 1992 791.43'75'0207—dc20
               92-23506
               CIP

DEDICATION

For Effie, who loved writers and taught me to love writing; and for
Leon K., who loves the movies.

CONTENTS

ACKNOWLEDGMENTS

Any publishing effort goes far beyond the name on its cover. So many people are part of the creation of the *FILM FLUBS* series that it would be impossible to list and thank them all without a separate volume devoted to that task alone. A special thanks to all of the wonderful people— named and unnamed—who wrote or stopped us on the street to tell us about their favorite movie gaffes (see Endnote, Page 150). Thanks to Nancy Yost, Barbara Lowenstein, Bart Andrews, Al Marill, Gail Kinn, Ben Petrone, Steven Schragis, and all the people at Carol Publishing Group for their hard work on these books. Thanks are also due to *Today's* Katie Couric and her staff for making an interview such a pleasant experience, especially when the writer is harried after the airline lost the very clothes he was to wear on the show; to the hundreds of radio talk show hosts and their call-in guests who've turned *FILM FLUBS* into one of their hottest topics; to the radio and television news and magazine shows who've built interesting stories around these books; to the newspaper and magazine reviewers and feature writers who've been so kind to our efforts; to the staff of the Margaret Herrick Library at the Academy of Motion Picture Arts and Sciences, the American Film Institute Library, Collectors Book Store, Larry Edmonds Bookshop, Video West, Craig Phillips, Christopher Kush, and of course, Leon and Rosebud—without whom none of this would be possible.

A special tip of the hat to all of the film buffs who work for book shops, video stores, and other retailers who've told their customers about *FILM FLUBS* books and made them best-sellers.

FOREWORD

This book and its predecessors are the products of incredible generosity—that of thousands of moviegoers who took the time and trouble to tell us about their favorite film flubs. It's been a real joy to read the letters we've received, ranging from remarkably intelligent flub-spotting by readers as young as nine years old to extensive compendiums of gaffes collected by others in a lifetime of movie watching.

The reception of the *FILM FLUBS* books by the movie industry has been truly gratifying and, at times, overwhelming. Good-natured, big-hearted professionals from every branch of the business have shared their favorites with us—even, at times, pointing out amusing flaws that slipped by them and appeared in their own work. Though we've taken some gentle potshots at just about every aspect of the movie business, there hasn't been one instance of "sour grapes" from anyone in the industry. It's the mark of true professionalism when you can enjoy a good laugh at your own expense.

FILM FLUBS and *SON OF FILM FLUBS* turned thousands of readers on to the fun of finding gaffes in their favorite movies, even to the point that some have written to tell us how much they enjoy the "new hobby" they've taken up after reading these books.

A delightful part of this experience has been hearing from people who found additional gaffes in films about which we've written before, or pointing out aspects of a particular flub that we hadn't realized.

An example of the former comes from *The Graduate* (1967). In *FILM FLUBS*, we pointed out that Dustin Hoffman is traveling the wrong way on San Francisco's Bay Bridge en route to Berkeley. A reader wrote to add to the story—that earlier in the film, when Hoffman is southbound, returning from Berkeley, he drives through a tunnel near Goleta, California. The tunnel is actually on the northbound side of the road. Ol' Benjamin Braddock is going the wrong way again. *FILM FLUBS* redux.

Readers have also showed us that flubbery can repeat and repeat itself. In *Adventures of Don Juan* (1948), Errol Flynn kisses Viveca Lindfors, and when they pull apart, a string of spittle remains between them. Again, in *The Prodigal* (1955), it happens during a kiss between Edmund Purdom and Lana Turner. Then, more recently, when Warren Beatty kisses a dying Madonna in *Dick Tracy* (1990), there's that string of drool again. Sloppy bussing to the third power.

Other readers have alerted us to delightful stories about the making of certain films, filled us in on the lives and works of great filmmakers, and even contributed delectable bits of film ephemera. An example is Greg

Donio's citation of a bit of doggerel about the lack of historical veracity in the works of Cecil B. DeMille. He tells us that critic James Agee was fond of quoting this verse, of anonymous authorship:

Cecil B. DeMille
Much Against His Will
Was Persuaded to Keep Moses
Out of the Wars of the Roses

Our sincerest appreciation to all of the wonderful people who continue to share their favorites. Some didn't make the cut purely for space reasons; others bear further investigation; still others turned out to be not quite what they seem. An example is a possible flub in *The Two Jakes* (1990). While it's true that Jack Nicholson walks out of the door of a tract housing office with his coat open and in the next shot closed, one person noticed that a tie clip appeared to come and go several times during the scene. A frame-by-frame examination revealed that what appeared to be a flub wasn't; it was Nicholson's tie flipping over in the breeze, revealing the label on the back. But it certainly looked like a flub, and we were delighted to hear about it.

When we wrote *FILM FLUBS*, while high hopes abounded, we had no idea that it would kick off what appears to be a new mini-pastime—finding amusing little flaws in major motion pictures. It has grown to *SON OF FILM FLUBS* and now *FILM FLUBS, THE SEQUEL*. As long as there continue to be readers who enjoy the *FILM FLUBS* series—and as long as you continue to share your favorites with us—we'll keep assembling these collections.

FILM FLUBS

The Sequel

INTRODUCTION

In previous books in the series, we discussed at length the hows and whys of film flubbery and the causes for their ultimate appearance on the screen. Rather than tread the same ground again, we commend the previous tomes to your attention (now there's a sneaky way to sell books!). In each we've tried to look at some aspect of the factors which make things go awry on films. However, there are topics which should bear discussion.

Film flubs can be more than the physical glitches which you see on screen. To many of us who have some subjective interest, anything that pulls us away from the story on the screen and into reality can, in truth, be classified as a flub.

My personal *bête noir* is botched accents, especially Southern ones. As a former Southerner who hasn't quite lost the sound, I groan, gripe, and grind my teeth when I see some ill-prepared actor try to fit a "grits and gravy" Southern accent into a mouth which can't quite hold it. I'd rather see them go for their own natural speech pattern. Adding insult to injury is the refuge of the brain-dead filmmaker who uses a Southern accent as the cliché to telegraph stupid, racist, or less than savory characters. I'm sure the folks from Brooklyn have to endure similar anguish.

Another personal gripe is the way presents are wrapped in movies and television shows. Perhaps to avoid rewraps for take after take, a gift given cinematically usually has a beribboned lid wrapped separately from the bottom, so it slides off carefully. In real life, of course, we rip, tear, and crumple the wrapping paper and box to get to the gift. We've never given nor received gifts wrapped as they are on film.

Elizabeth Taylor is the queen of bad Southern accents—see *Cat on a Hot Tin Roof* (1958) or *Raintree County* (1957) as examples. Joe Pesci's Southern accent in *JFK* (1991) is so bad that you want to laugh at the parts which really aren't funny—and Kevin Costner's in the same film is such a distraction that you wonder if he has a clue about vocal technique (see also *Robin Hood*). New Orleans residents were not amused when Costner's *JFK* accent wasn't theirs with its Cajun overtones, but a drawl more common to Mississippi and Alabama.

Another big-time annoyance is the constant use of wet streets in night shots—especially in films taking place in Los Angeles. I know why they do it—the shiny surface makes for better reflections and a more pleasing shot. But as a Los Angeles resident, I have to tell you that the streets here are wet probably less than ten nights a year. Every time I see damp pavement in a scene set in L.A., my attention is diverted from the on-screen story.

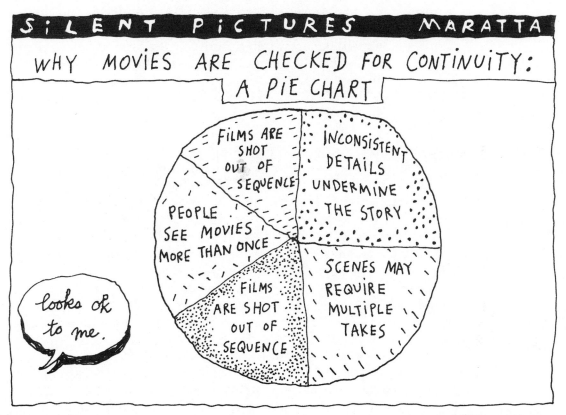

While I'm on the shrink's couch, indulge me as I point out one other filmic technique which bugs me, even though it's certainly not a flub. But is it possible to end a movie without a traditional pullback, the camera moving into a panoramic view of the scene as our heroes walk, run, drive, fly, ride on horseback, or stumble into the horizon? There's almost always a road in the shot, heading straight over a slight rise into infinity. Is this something that directors learn, with the technique being passed down from one generation to another, or is it merely a colossal lack of imagination? Your call.

Misplaced geography is another bothersome distraction, especially to one living in the area where a movie was filmed. You may not have noticed the pan from downtown L.A. to downtown San Francisco in *The Doctor* (see page 29), but many of us Los Angeleans were jarred by it. In the same vein, we didn't notice the geographic blunders in *No Way Out* (page 31), but Washingtonians did, being especially bugged by Costner's use of a Georgetown MetroRail station. There's no station in Georgetown. But again, it's hard to classify these as flubs, since location shooting has its own set of exigencies. Many times, license must be taken.

Nonetheless, Austrians were amused when *The Sound of Music* (1965) was first shown in their country, because as the Von Trapp family made its way across the mountains to freedom, in reality they were heading straight into Nazi Germany.

Then again, location gaffes are not endemic to the movies. In the opera *Manon Lescaut*, Puccini exiles his heroine to the desert just outside New Orleans. Go find it—or go figure.

Yet another on-screen flub that has bothered me for years is the camera's iris reflection—that little pentagram that flashes onto the screen when the camera is pointed directly at the sun. I'm happy to report that I have a cohort in this one. Allan Provost wrote to *The Hollywood Reporter* to kvetch about the same subject, putting it succinctly: "Why is it that so many filmmakers allow sunspots, dramatic streaks of light and even the concentric circles caused by the camera to dominate scenes? The effect is the same as seeing the microphone boom: It reminds the viewer of the technology and ruins the sense of involvement."

We especially enjoyed his reflection (oops! unintentional pun) on *Black Robe* which, he says, "has gone to great lengths to create the sense of looking at a bygone world and then, by golly, ending it with the visible lens, reminding me that my intense concern for the cold and starving Indians was unfounded, since they were just a short distance away from the jelly doughnuts of the nearest catering truck."

A reader pointed out something which never occurred to us, but now that we think about it—j'ever notice that in movies, almost everyone at the on-screen funeral wears black, whereas in real life, hardly anyone does these days? And that frequently, there's a carved tombstone in place before the body's even cold? Yet another cinematic cliché.

End of sermon. Pass the plate. Let the flubbing begin.

NOW YOU SEE IT, NOW YOU DON'T

Today's "reality" television shows have a field day when they come up with mysterious disappearances. Let us not fall behind the trends. We have some of our own. But, unlike those guys, we're not going to leave you in the lurch. We have some answers.

More often than not, dis- and re-appearances are the result of nonsequential shooting. A prop, an item of clothing, or some other object is photographed on one day, and the next day, or even weeks later, it manages not to get back into the shot. Or, even more interesting, someone mixes up the action sequences and cuts in footage that includes something that shouldn't have appeared until later in the film—an inadvertent precurser of things yet to come.

Such was the case in *One Good Cop* (1991) when a confusion of footage or shooting schedules or who knows what caused Anthony LaPaglia, playing Michael Keaton's partner, to awaken in bed with a nasty cut across his nose. The next time we see him, on the job with Keaton, the cut is gone. Since there hadn't been enough time for it to heal, what happened? It turns out that a few minutes later, when the cops do battle with three toughs in an elevator, LaPaglia gets the cut.

Or there's the forgotten prop, as was the case in *City Slickers* (1991) when Jack Palance is buried on the plains. There are flowers on Palance's grave as Billy Crystal and the other wannabe cowboys stand around it, but moments later, as they walk away, the flowers are gone. Was the crusty Palance upset over his stolen flowers? Is that why he made that rude remark when accepting his Oscar for his role as surly Curly, giving Billy Crystal fodder for an entire evening's worth of jokes?

Did Phil Joanou Build a Carwash Near the Golden Gate?

When Richard Gere's character drives up to the lighthouse in *Final Analysis* (1992), the car gets stuck in a muddy rut. There's much wheel spinning, splattering mud and water on the back of the car. But when Gere gets out of the rut (something that many films never really do), the car has cleaned itself up nicely. Then again, much of the action takes place in a lighthouse, with the Golden Gate Bridge visible nearby. Ain't so. There's no lighthouse there. It's a special effects creation, an invention of director Phil Joanou.

Tiny Footprints on the Shirt

Either they had come up with the formula for disappearing paint, or there was a laundromat in Never-Never Land. In *Hook* (1991), when a grown-up Peter Pan (Robin Williams) arrives there, the Lost Boys shoot him with plungers filled with a fluid that stains his shirt. Then Tinker Bell (Julia Roberts) walks all over him, literally. When he returns home, he still has the tiny footprints on his shirt, but the stains are gone.

And while we're speaking of things that vanish, did you notice that the family flies to England on Pan Am Airways, which had itself disappeared by the time the movie was released?

In Your Face, Jack

Jack Lemmon listens to Dorothy Provine's song in a barroom scene in *The Great Race* (1965). He's evidently been holding his mug of beer for quite a while, since even though it's full, there's no head on it. At one point during the song, Provine turns Lemmon around, and now there's a thick head on the beer, which she then blows in his face.

Did They Steal Tom Cruise's Famous Jockey Shorts, Too?

During one of the final scenes of *Risky Business* (1983), a moving van can be seen filled with furniture. But it appears that someone made a quick heist. As the van drives away, it is empty.

Food and the Beast

Food must be in the eyes of the beholder. There's a scene in *Beauty and the Beast* (1991) when the Beast gets food on his face while having trouble with table manners. But when Belle ("Beauty") looks at him, he's clean. Then the food's back again. Food also comes and goes from Ogre's face during a pie-eating scene in *Revenge of the Nerds* (1984). Gosh, you try and try to teach Beasts and Ogres good manners and what thanks do you get?

Beauty and the Books

Something also happens to the first book that Belle puts in her basket in the aforementioned *Beauty and the Beast* (1991). It disappears. Yet when a lamb bites a piece from another book, the bite pops right back in— shades of Julia Robert's gambit with the pancake in *Pretty Woman* (1990).

23

Missing Oranges

About halfway through *Out of Africa* (1985), while on a camping trip, Meryl Streep and Robert Redford are sitting around a campfire during a night scene and he's peeling an orange. Even though it appears that he's peeling only one, the number of oranges in the bowl on the camp table keeps changing.

The Panther Stole It

David Niven tries to seduce Claudia Cardinale on a tigerskin rug in *The Pink Panther* (1964). Her cigarette changes from one hand to another, then disappears entirely as they kiss.

Licking the Lost Child

One of the saddest disappearances happens in *Bambi* (1942). When the animals are on the other side of the river after having fled the forest fire, a mother raccoon licks her baby—then it vanishes, leaving her licking the air. But in another instance, there's a mother-and-child reunion when Bambi's mom is leading him through the wilderness. She momentarily disappears, then reappears again. Still another loss occurs when a flock of crows is flying across the screen and about eight of them simply vanish.

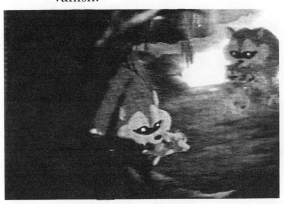

No Chocaholic, He

Fred Astaire gets rid of a box of candy in *Holiday Inn* (1942) by throwing it over the back of a park bench. It lands on the ground next to a planter only to disappear and reappear again.

The Changing Family Dynamic

A real case of "now you see it, now you don't" happens in Jane Fonda and Robert De Niro's *Stanley and Iris* (1990). Two characters—Iris's sister Sharon (Swoosie Kurtz) and Sharon's husband Joe (Jamey Sheridan)—disappear halfway through the picture, without explanation. Turns out that it was due to the director's changing his mind about the family dynamic. Director Martin Ritt told Rob Medich in *Premiere* magazine that he cut them out because of a scene where Sharon finds her husband having sex with Iris's daughter Kelly (Martha Plimpton). He wanted to change the way things worked within the family. Now that's an understatement!

Sleigh Bells Ring/Don't Ring, Are You Listening?

When the reindeer is released at the end of *Prancer* (1990), first it's wearing sleigh bells, then it isn't, then it is again.

A Quick Cleanup in a Galaxy Far, Far Away

The cup of tea which Captain Sulu (George Takai) drinks in *Star Trek VI* (1991) crashes to the floor when the spaceship is attacked. Sulu falls also, but by the time he gets up, the cleanup crew must have made a fast trip onto the set, because the pieces of the shattered cup and saucer have vanished.

Noah Gets Lost

A character disappears during the course of the classic *The Grapes of Wrath* (1940). Tom Joad (Henry Fonda) has a semi-retarded younger brother Noah (Frank Sully) who is part of the story up until the swimming-in-the-river scene after which we never see him again. In the book Noah feels he's a burden and runs away; in the movie, there's no explanation for his disappearance.

GEOGRAPHY LESSONS

The nature of filmmaking is such that one city is often used to simulate another, or that a car can turn a corner in one side of town and end up miles away. To the residents of the area where the movie was filmed, it's fairly jarring, but to audiences who haven't been there, there's no reason to notice. Residents of Los Angeles, New York, and other cities which are frequent filming sites are usually enured to such happenstances, since we just assume that there was a good reason for the seamless transition from one part of town to another.

But some geographical gaffes are fairly obvious, such as the appearance of major mountains in Fort Smith, Arkansas, in *True Grit* (1969). The locals saw it and said, "No way." Likewise, many a Chicagoan noticed that when Billy Crystal and Meg Ryan leave the University of Chicago in *When Harry Met Sally* (1989), there's a bit of a local geography problem. The university is on the city's south side; yet when they leave the campus, they're next seen heading south on North Lake Shore Drive. They're heading right back to the campus. Perhaps they forgot something?

Chicagoans also had a bit of a problem with *Planes, Trains, and Automobiles* (1989), when John Candy and Steve Martin approach Chicago from the south and the landmark Sears Tower and the Presidential Towers are in the positions that they would be seen in from the north. Director John Hughes should know better. It's his hometown. And when Candy and Martin pulled over in the burned car en route to Chicago from St. Louis, they're stopped by a Wisconsin State Trooper. They must be taking the scenic route.

Near the end, when the mismatched traveling companions enter a train and it leaves the station, you can see two sets of tracks. After pondering his relationship with Candy, Martin returns on the train to the station on the same track, but exits on the same platform he just left. We're talking a fast round-trip. Or was it just a matter of running the film in reverse? Evidence exists: You can see a person walking backward on the street below the station.

One Hell of a Lens

Even though *The Doctor* (1992) is set in San Francisco, as William Hurt and Elizabeth Perkins converse on the roof of an office building, several downtown Los Angeles high-rises can be seen in the background, most noticeably the Library Tower. Then the camera pans around the horizon, where we can now see San Francisco's Bay Bridge. Considering that the two cities are about five hundred miles apart, the cinematographer must have used a marvelous lens on a magnificently clear day.

Same for You, Dick

We're happy to report that Richard Gere brought things full circle in *Final Analysis* (1992). He exits the *San Francisco* courthouse via the steps of *Los Angeles* City Hall. As an aside, your flubmeister was enroute to a meeting inside City Hall when that particular scene was being shot and had to sidestep the production crew. Little did I know at the time that I was present at the birth of a flub!

Perhaps We Could Call It San Franangeles

Then again, perhaps Hollywood is trying to prepare us for the scientific prediction that when The Big One hits, the tectonic plate slip is going to draw San Francisco and L.A. closer together. In *Predator II*, what is supposed to be a Los Angeles subway has cars marked "BART"...that being the acronym for the San Francisco's Bay Area Rapid Transit system.

The Lost Brigade

History buffs won't let *Glory* (1989) get away with its wrong-way march. As the 54th advances on Fort Wagner, the Atlantic Ocean is on their left, meaning that they attacked from the north. Wrong. In the actual battle, they advanced from south to north, so the ocean should be on their right.

And a Flub Is Still a Flub

"An airport is an airport." That's what a spokesman for Castle Rock Entertainment told *People* magazine when that journal wondered why, in *City Slickers* (1991), Billy Crystal, supposedly being met by his family in New York, actually arrives at the Bradley Terminal at Los Angeles International (LAX). Many, many flub spotters wondered, too, even though one of the LAX direction signs in the background had been changed to read "New York Helicopter." The production was based in L.A., and Castle Rock wanted to avoid the expense of flying the actors to New York to film the brief scene, just as did the producers of *Big Business* (1988), as reported in *FILM FLUBS*.

Not Knowing Your Way Around Washington

Washington is the setting for *No Way Out* (1987). But even though filmmakers often (usually, in fact) take geographical liberties with location shooting, nonetheless locals noticed that even though Kevin Costner boards the subway in Georgetown, there's no stop there. In fact, the subway used in one of the chase scenes is not in Washington at all; it's in Baltimore. And a newspaper reporter pointed out that to get to Annapolis for a romantic weekend, you don't make a lovely drive down the scenic George Washington Parkway—as did Costner and Sean Young. Instead, you have to travel through a grungy part of the city. Also, they're heading west on the Parkway, which would mean that they'd have a lovely weekend at the CIA.

31

Misplacing Miss Daisy

When Hoke (Morgan Freeman) takes Miss Daisy (Jessica Tandy) into Alabama in *Driving Miss Daisy* (1989), he tells her that it's his first time outside of Georgia. But when they're met by patrolmen after they've crossed the state line, the officers are wearing Georgia State Trooper shoulder patches. An alert Georgian also noticed that not only does Hoke drive past the same house with the same truck in front of it *twice* in fifteen seconds on the way home from temple, but when he brings Miss Daisy coffee from the Krispy Kreme, it's in a styrofoam cup—something that didn't exist in the late 1950s.

Misplaced Wildlife

Tarzan and the Trappers (1958) opens with a description of Guatemala, followed by shots of zebras, giraffes, lions, and other African animals.

The Bird Is a Traveling Turkey

A prime example of a geographical misadventure occurs in the Mel Gibson–Goldie Hawn starrer, *Bird on a Wire* (1990). Come to think of it, the very making of this movie was a misadventure. Let us talk "turkey." The couple leaves Detroit and takes a ferry to Racine, Wisconsin. As *Premiere* magazine's Terri Minsky points out, it's the kind of journey that would take a Magellan. If there were a ferry from Detroit to Racine, it would have to take the Detroit River to Lake St. Clair, continue on via the St. Clair River to Lake Huron, go all the way up Lake Huron and traverse into Lake Michigan, traveling about two-thirds of the way down to Racine. The trip would take several days at best.

Terminator II: Judgment Day

In each book, we award the "Flubbie" to a movie which earns the dubious distinction of "Flubbed-Up Movie of the Year." In 1990, it was *Pretty Woman*. The 1991 award was won hands-down by *Terminator II: Judgment Day*.

As a bit of a caveat, having read much about the making of *T2*, we have to admit that as one of filmdom's great displays of special effects wizardry, it was a real bear to make—and the wonder is that it did get put together, and that it does work. The efforts of hundreds of technicians from dozens of companies had to come together in one motion picture, and that there is any continuity at all is a tribute to the film-makers. But, as Marc Antony said, we did not come here to praise. Our task is to point out flubs, and we shall not shirk it.

Early on, a couple of flubs pop up. When Arnie is heading toward the bar, he passes a car parked outside. His cranial read-out says that the car he's scanning is a Plymouth Sedan. But those who know say that it's a Ford.

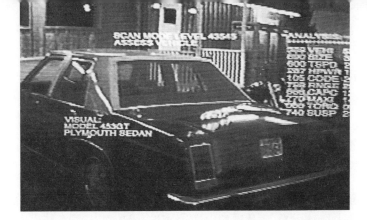

Then he goes into the bar, where a denizen burns a hole in his chest with a cigar. But as the cigar is pulled away, the burn disappears for a brief moment before returning in the next shot.

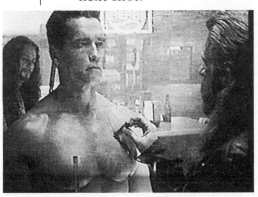 

A couple of errors even dog Linda Hamilton. As she runs down a hospital hallway barefoot, you hear the pitter-patter of feet wearing shoes. A little glitch from the Foley stage.

Later, she tells the doctor that there are 215 bones in the human body. He should have corrected her—there are only 206. Another thing about this sequence bothered many viewers—if she's in a high-security hospital, how could she get out with something as simple as a paper clip?

The film is plagued with examples of glass breaking out then popping right back in. One of the most obvious happens when Robert Patrick, as the "bad" Terminator, drives the heavy wrecker over the bridge into the Los Angeles River—yep, that's what it really is; that's the best we can do for a river out here!

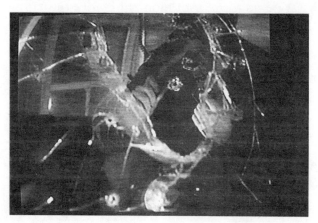

Notice that as the truck hits the pavement, both windshields pop out. But in the very next shot, as the chase continues, they're back in place, albeit cracked. The glass broken out of the guard shack at the hospital by Arnie also returns in a later shot, as does a rear window in the police van as they're being chased by a helicopter. And while we're at it, in a close-up you can see a hole blown in the helicopter's windshield. In a later long shot, the hole's gone.

When Schwarzenegger, as the "good" Terminator, and young Edward Furlong are in the parking lot and Furlong tells him to put the gun down, he does so on his right side. But when Furlong picks the gun up, it has moved closer to the other side.

When Robert Patrick transforms into Furlong's foster *mother*, he kills the foster *father* with his left arm that's been turned into a blade. But when he falls into the molten metal and "rewinds" through his various transformations, Patrick's right arm is the blade.

Speaking of the molten metal sequence, an electrician noted that when she lowers Arnold into the soup, Linda Hamilton pushes the button on the control panel that would normally raise him up rather than lower him. Was this a last-ditch rescue attempt?

We close with our favorite *T2* flub: look closely as Robert Patrick chases the police van in the helicopter. A couple of times when he's using both hands to reload his gun, you see an extra hand sneak out to fly the helicopter. We know he could transform himself, but an extra hand? It's surely the real-life helicopter pilot.

While we're at it, we have to report a few flubs from the first Terminator movie. We received several letters pointing out problems as the characters moved from one film to the next—young John Connor's ages, script logic, etc. However, we have to realize that these are fictional works, and trying to tie an original and a sequel together is putting just a bit too much reality into an unreal product.

However, in *The Terminator* (1984), a few funnies did pop up. For one, Linda Hamilton goes to a pay phone to call the police because she's being followed. She puts a quarter in and dials 911. She didn't have to do that; 911 calls do not require a coin deposit.

Schwarzenegger tries to locate Linda Hamilton's character, Sarah Connor, by looking up her name in the phone book. There are three Sarah Connors, with addresses beginning with 1823, 2816, and 309. Arnie tries to eliminate them methodically, but when he arrives at the home of the first one, it's 14239. Was there madness in his method?

When he walks into a police station looking for Sarah, he talks briefly to a cop, recites the famous "I'll be back" line, then leaves. The cop returns to his paperwork, then is caught in the glare of headlights as the Terminator's car crashes into the station. The cop is shown again, still in the headlights. But when the car crashes in, the headlights are off.

GIVING CREDITS THEIR DUE

The opening and closing credits of movies are rife with opportunities for the flub spotter with an eye for the awry. There's no telling what you'll find when you do your own credit check—misspellings, characters who weren't in the film but got a screen credit anyway, and all sorts of other surprises. Feast your eyes on some recently-unearthed favorites:

They're Not Who You Think They Are

Abbott and Costello call each other by their real names—"Bud" and "Lou"—throughout *Abbott and Costello Meet the Mummy* (1955). But the closing credits identify Bud as playing "Pete Patterson" and Louis as "Freddie Franklin."

March-ing to the Beat of a Different Speller

Fredric March had a lot of trouble keeping his professional moniker under control in the credits. Misspellings popped up in several films. Look for it in the end credits of *The Best Years of Our Lives* (1946), where his name's spelled "Frederic." Then, years later, it happens all over again in *Mr. and Mrs. Bridge* (1990), where his name once more turns up as "Frederick" on a movie poster. Elsewhere in the same credits, bandleader Glenn Miller becomes "Glen."

They Couldn't Tell Each Other Apart

Not even the great *Gone With the Wind* (1939) is without its credits problems, taking us into an interesting realm. It's normal for most of us to have difficulty telling which twin is which. But is it also a problem for the twins themselves? George Reeves, who later became Superman, played one of the Tarleton twins and is identified in the opening credits as "Brent." However, when the twins talk with Scarlett O'Hara about the upcoming barbecue at Twelve Oaks, Reeves points to his twin brother (Fred Crane) and calls him "Brent."

Recalling the Error

When Disney's *Fantasia* (1940) was restored and rereleased in 1990, some of the early prints had to be recalled to correct a spelling error on Leopold Stokowski's name in the opening credits.

For the 'L' Of It

In *Total Recall* (1990), story credit is given to sci-fi novelist "Phillip K. Dick." It's "Philip," with one "L."

At Least It's Still Alliterative

Throughout the film, Melanie Griffith's character in *Pacific Heights* (1990) is called either "Patty Palmer" or "Patricia Palmer," yet in the closing credits, she's identified as "Patricia Parker."

Let's See…That's "I" Before "E" Except After "C," or Is It?

Sean Connery's character in *Outland* (1981) is spelled "O'Niel" on a computer screen in the movie, as well as in the end credits. But on his name tag, it's "O'Neil."

And She Made Such a Point of It, Too

Steve Martin's oh-so-L.A. girlfriend, Sarah Jessica Parker, in *L.A. Story* (1991) makes a big deal of the spelling of her name as "SanDee." Yet in the closing credits, it's "Sandy." Well, she tried.

41

A Field Demotion or a Rank Error?

In the title credits of *The Wolf Man* (1941), Ralph Bellamy is identified as playing "Colonel Mumford." In the first five minutes of the film, Claude Rains is talking to Lon Chaney, Jr., and refers to Bellamy as "Captain Mumford."

Credit Me Back to Old Virginia

Here's a real switch. The original one-sheet poster for *That Lady in Ermine* (1948) gave actor Reginald Gardiner an inadvertent sex change. His name on the poster, for some unexplained reason, was "Virginia Gardiner."

Katharine Lost Her A's in the Deal

Hard as she tried over six decades of stardom, Katharine Hepburn had a devil of a time getting her name spelled correctly in the credits. It was Katherine Hepburn in *A Bill of Divorcement* (1932), just as it was again in *State of the Union* (1948).

You're Nobody 'Til Somebody Loves You

Who's the hottest kid in show business since Shirley Temple? Macauley Culkin, of course. He made an appearance in a minor but significant role in *Jacob's Ladder* (1990), as Tim Robbins's son. But since it was filmed prior to his success in *Home Alone* (1990), Culkin's name doesn't appear in the credits.

More of the Name Game

The Hollywood Reporter columnist Robert Osborne has found that on the box for the videocassette release of *Demetrius and the Gladiators* (1954), Susan Hayward was identified as "Susan Hayworth." Someone must have gotten their redheads mixed up. But that certainly wasn't a first (or the last, we're sure). Osborne's *Daily Variety* competitor, Army Archerd, says that on screening cassettes of *Reversal of Fortune* sent to the Academy Award voters last year, Glenn Close's name was spelled "Glen" and director Barbet Schroeder's as "Shroeder."

And a Few Closing Comments...

Many a director likes to slip a few jokes into the closing credits. In *Ferris Bueller's Day Off* (1986), at the end of the credit crawl, Matthew Broderick reappears on the screen to ask, "Why are you still here? Go home!" or something to that effect. Several Burt Reynolds films show outtakes during the credit crawl, adding a bit of laughter to the list of names of people known, more often than not, only to their friends who worked on the picture and to their respective mothers.

The credits can even be provocative, as in *The Mission* (1986) where, if you'll wait until the end, you'll see the Bishop make a reappearance which seems to indicate that he's not at all sure of the correctness of his actions in the film.

End credit jokes can backfire, too. Outtakes showing Peter Sellers giggling and breaking character absolutely destroy the magic created just a few moments before in *Being There* (1979).

But the ZAZ team—Zucker/Abrahams/Zucker—takes the end credit spoofing to a new high. *Airplane!* (1980) lists "Author of *A Tale of Two Cities:* Charles Dickens" in its credits. In *Airplane II* (1982), right after the credit for "Best Boy," we get "Worst Boy: Adolph Hitler." In *Top Secret!* (1984), we see "Hey Diddle Diddle...The Cat and the Fiddle."

Ruthless People (1986) credits "Best Boy: Victor Perez" followed by "Best Pitcher: Dwight Gooden." In *The Naked Gun* (1988) there's "Dolly Grip: Jon Falkengren," "Poli-Grip: Martha Raye," "What the Hell Is a Grip? Person Responsible for Maintenance and Adjustment to Equipment on the Set."

Perhaps best of all are Abrahams's closing credits jokes in *Hot Shots!* (1991). Not only do you get a recipe for brownies and nobby buns, but there's also a list of suggestions for things to do after the movie, including "Help Someone Learn to Read" and "Visit a dairy and see how milk is handled and prepared for delivery."

At the end of the *Hot Shots!* credit crawl, you'll see "If you had left this theater when the credits began, you'd be home now."

And in *Lethal Weapon III*, if you wait out the credits, you'll see yet another building explosion and a possible setup for *LW IV*.

See what you missed?

INSIDE JOKES

Ever since Alfred Hitchcock started the business of making cameo appearances in his own films—perhaps even before—directors, writers, and actors have loved to slip little "inside jokes" into their movies. More often than not, they're either subtle tributes or gentle digs at their friends in the business, references to their own earlier works, sight gags, or unbilled cameos of themselves and their buddies.

An inside joke can fit into the definition of a film flub—something that adds a quick dose of reality to the fantasy which is being played out on the screen—but unlike the accidents and oversights which make up most of the *FILM FLUBS* collections, inside jokes are intentional and deliberate.

Steven Spielberg and George Lucas love the in-joke so much that often they seem to trade little tributes to each other's work. Spielberg's *Indiana Jones and the Temple of Doom* (1984) opens with a sequence in Hong Kong's Club Obi-Wan. Think about it. In *Raiders of the Lost Ark* (1981) Indy is rescued by a seaplane bearing the license number OB-CPO, a nudge at the *Star Wars* characters. Also in *Raiders* there's an in-joke you'll have to look for in the movie houses, since it's too small to be seen on video. But when the Ark is moved, C3PO and R2D2 supposedly appear in the hieroglyphics on the Wall of Souls.

In *Close Encounters of the Third Kind* (1977) a minuscule R2D2 is built into the superstructure of the mothership. Spielberg is also fond of recalling his earlier works, as in *Gremlins* (1984). He executive-produced

45

the film, and on a theater marquee could be seen the titles *A Boy's Life* and *Watch the Skies*—the working titles for *E. T. The Extra-Terrestrial* and *Close Encounters of the Third Kind*.

George Lucas isn't above the in-joke, too. The license plate number in *American Graffiti* (1973) is "THX-1138," the title of Lucas's first feature (and also the patronym of THX, his theatrical sound system). A cell block in *Star Wars* (1977) bears the same number. It's apparently meaningless. Lucas told an interviewer he just likes the sound of it.

There seems to be a bit of an in-joke in *Return of the Jedi* (1983). An alert viewer spotted a flying shoe in outer space. During a battle scene, Lando looks up from his controls and out of the Falcon's window a shoe moves from top left to bottom right. We've heard that there's a lot of garbage in outer space. Is Lucas confirming that for us?

"See You" in the Movies

Director John Landis likes to slip the phrase "See you next Wednesday" in his movies. It pops up in *Kentucky Fried Movie* (1977), *The Blues Brothers* (1980), *An American Werewolf in London* (1981), *Amazon Women on the Moon* (1987), and *Coming to America* (1988). The phrase is written in blood in the Landis-directed Michael Jackson video, *Thriller* (1984). Landis himself becomes the butt of a sick in-joke in *Wired* (1989). As the actor portraying the director walks across *The Blues Brothers* set, the sound of helicopters can be heard in the background. If you don't know what that's referring to, you don't know movies.

Targeting the Critics

On the set of *Willow* (1988), the two-headed monster was known as the "Ebersisk," a reference to Siskel and Ebert, even though the name didn't appear in the film. But critic Pauline Kael was speared in the same film by having the Evil General Kael bear her name.

The Road to the Circus

When Dorothy Lamour appears on-screen in *The Greatest Show on Earth* (1952), her "Road" buddies Bob Hope and Bing Crosby are sitting among the popcorn munching crowd on the circus bleachers.

Doing It Like a Rabbit

Some animation fans think that a quickie inside joke was drawn into *The Wabbit Who Came to Dinner.* In a scene where Bugs emerges from the shower and wraps a towel around himself (itself a bit of an oddity since he usually didn't wear clothes), there's a frame or two where an added bit of anatomy that you don't see in other "Bugs" cartoons seems to appear between his legs.

The Subliminal Dig

In John Carpenter's debut film, *Dark Star* (1974), for a brief moment on one of the computer screens appears the message, "Fuck You, Harris." Seems Carpenter didn't get along too well with the film's producer, Jack H. Harris.

Everybody Has to Start Somewhere

In *Bananas* (1971) look for an unknown player to practice his pugilistic skills by mugging Woody Allen on a New York subway. The same actor gets his just desserts in *Prisoner of Second Avenue* (1975), when, as an alleged pickpocket, he's mugged by Jack Lemmon. The neophyte bit player is Sylvester Stallone.

Paying Homage to the Family

Among the names which Dustin Hoffman memorizes and recites in *Rain Man* (1988) are Marsha and William Gottsegen—in real life, Hoffman's in-laws.

Paying Homage to One's Self

A radio station employee in Oliver Stone's *Talk Radio* (1988) reads a copy of *Playboy* which features an interview with…Oliver Stone.

Paying Homage to One's Work

Child actors sing the theme from Alan Parker's *Fame* (1980) and a poster featuring Parker's *Pink Floyd—The Wall* (1982) appears in Parker's *Shoot the Moon* (1982). Incidentally, *The Wall* wasn't released until five months after *Shoot the Moon*. But Parker isn't the only one. In *Lethal Weapon* (1987) Richard Donner advertises his upcoming movie with a theater marquee in the background which reads "*The Lost Boys*—This Year's Hit."

Paying Homage to the Progenitors

In *2010* (1984), the man feeding the pigeons on a park bench outside the White House is *2001/2010* writer Arthur C. Clarke. Clarke also appears on the cover of *Time* magazine as the President of the United States, alongside another familiar face as premier of the USSR—director Stanley Kubrick.

Kubrick himself pulls off an in-joke by displaying a copy of the *2001: A Space Odyssey* sound track in a record shop in *A Clockwork Orange* (1971).

While we're on the subject, did you know that the very date in *2001* that the computer HAL says that he became operational is itself a flub? Hal says that it was January 12, 1992—but in an interview published on that date, Clarke himself says that it was a flub.

He told the *Los Angeles Times* "…the strange thing is that in the book it's 1997—not 1992—and I have no idea when the change occurred, whether Stanley [Kubrick] changed it in the screenplay [coauthored by Clarke] or the actor flubbed his line."

Welcome, Mr. Clarke, to our Blue-Ribbon Flub Spotter Panel.

Homage to One's Own Work: The Sequel

When the camera tracks down a New York street in *Ghostbusters II* (1989), notice the theater marquee advertising *Cannibal Girls* starring director Ivan Reitman's buddies Eugene Levy and Andrea Martin. The advertised movie was a 1973 Canadian cheapie, an early effort of Reitman, Levy, and Martin.

The Sign of Capra-Corn

Director Frank Capra, whose heartwarming, feel-good films were often directed with a "Capra-corn" label, created a signature for himself when he first used a raven in *You Can't Take It With You* (1938). The bird appeared in each of his subsequent films, including a starring role as Uncle Billy's pet "Jimmy" in *It's a Wonderful Life* (1946).

51

ILL LOGIC

In just about every interview we've done—and there have been literally hundreds—one question pops up time and again: "What's your favorite film flub?" That's like asking which is your favorite child—we love 'em all. But if there is a particular *type* of flub that we enjoy the most, it would have to be those that we categorize as "Ill Logic." These are the flubs that happen when the thought processes go slightly awry. Someone doesn't think about what they are saying, doing, or writing into the script; or artistic license is taken a bit to the other side of our suspension of disbelief.

For instance:

Springtime in January

In the opening credit sequence of *Born on the Fourth of July* (1989), a young Ron Kovic runs home on a sunny day. There are leaves on the trees, and the kids are dressed casually. When he gets home, he sits with the family and watches John F. Kennedy's inaugural speech on TV. Since that happened on January 20, 1961, and the family lives on Long Island, shouldn't the trees be bare and perhaps some snow on the ground? Or was it just a very, mild winter?

A Point to Ponder

Adam (played by Michael Parks) has a navel in *The Bible* (1966). Think about it.

Where Does Real Stop and Surreal Begin?

In the last quarter of *Barton Fink* (1991), John Goodman tells John Turturro (as Fink) that he is leaving the hotel and doesn't know when he will return. Goodman takes two suitcases, says good-bye, and walks out. A day or two passes, and in the middle of typing a screenplay, Turturro opens the door and places his shoes in the hall for shining. Goodman's shoes are in front of the door to the room that he keeps permanently, even though he's gone.

Shedding a Little Light on the Subject

The electricity is off in a scene in *White Palace* (1990). So why does the light come on in the refrigerator when the door is opened? Hmmm…

The Kid Needs Sleep Therapy

When Michael Douglas tucks his daughter into bed for the night in *Fatal Attraction* (1987), he looks out the window. It's dark, but you can see that his watch reads about 3:15. It's either a very dreary day or the kid is going to bed at a really strange hour.

The little girl also does some high-speed aging. At one point in the movie Anne Archer says that the youngster is five years old; but later, when Glenn Close asks Michael Douglas he says that she's six. There certainly hadn't been enough time for her to age a year. Or did she have a birthday party and we weren't invited?

A Few More Months and She Could Have Birthed an Elephant

A critic once pointed out that if you time Melanie's pregnancy to the Civil War battles in *Gone With the Wind* (1939), she was pregnant for twenty-one months. Informed of the time discrepancy, author Margaret Mitchell once replied that Southerners always do things at a slower pace than Yankees.

The Gremlins Also Got in the Editing Room

In order to match a *Gremlins* (1984) long shot with a close-up, the film was run backwards for one scene. The gremlin had hot-wired a traffic light so that both directions showed green. However, the reversal makes the smoke and sparks jump *toward* the wires, an interesting twist on the laws of physics.

We've Never Had a Housekeeper This Fast

In the final moments of *The Time Machine* (1960), the housekeeper, who is alone in the house, closes the door after a departing Alan Young. Then we see both upstairs and downstairs lights go out in a matter of seconds. Did she zoom up the stairs, or did the house have a master switch?

A Modest Oprah

Oprah Winfrey is knocked out cold when pistol-whipped with the butt of a revolver in *The Color Purple* (1985). But when the wind blows up her skirt, the unconscious Oprah reaches out and pushes it back down.

A Not So Crystal Clear Case of Genetic Engineering

Now here's something to ponder concerning the "cow" that gives birth to the calf in *City Slickers* (1991). If Billy Crystal actually helped at the calving, he may well have been part of an event that made a bit of genetic history. Several farm-belt flub spotters will swear 'til the cows come home that the "mother" is a mixed-breed beef cow giving birth to a pure-bred Jersey dairy calf. It's a cinematic improbability and a genetic impossibility.

Santa Slips Up

Either director/screenwriter George Seaton or fabulist Valentine Davies didn't do his homework in *Miracle on 34th Street* (1947). Beloved Kris Kringle asks: "Who was Vice President under John Quincy Adams? Daniel D. Tompkins." Sorry, Santa. It was John C. Calhoun; Tompkins was James Monroe's Dan Quayle.

And Then He Went Off to the Confederate Air Force

John Wayne, playing Ethan Edwards, returns home in *The Searchers* (1956), visits his brother's family, and gives his niece a medal which was given to him by the Confederate government. Superpatriot Wayne must have coined it himself; the Confederates didn't give medals.

Stopping Planetary Time

A considerable amount of time goes by while the extraterrestrial is hiding in a shed in *E.T.* (1982), but the moon never moves.

Eyes in the Back of His Head

Gene Wilder plays a deaf character and Richard Pryor is blind in *See No Evil, Hear No Evil* (1989). In a scene where they are trying to rescue Pryor's kidnapped sister, they are stalking through the house when Pryor asks Wilder if his sister is okay. Wilder is looking away but answers him anyway. Think about it.

Reflections of a Film Flub

Count Dracula changes from a bat into Lon Chaney, Jr., in front of a mirror in *Son of Dracula* (1943). You know the business about a vampire casting no reflection? Things got a little backward. Dracula (here, "Count Alucard") is clearly seen in the mirror, but when he flies in as a bat, neither the bat nor the animated transformation appears in the mirror. Chaney's image pops in as soon as he's transformed.

An Innocent Mistake

Tom Selleck gets out of a car in *An Innocent Man* (1990) locking the door without noticing that the window is still down. He'd better hope that a guilty man doesn't notice how easy it would be to break into the car.

A Precursor of Things to Come

Here's another "point to ponder": in *The Ten Commandments* (1956), in a scene before the birth of Moses, an early Pharaoh decrees the slaughter of the Hebrew boys, announcing, "So says Ramses the First." Since the second didn't come along until about forty years later, shouldn't he have said "So says Ramses" and leave it at that?

Robin Hood: Prince of Thieves

Rarely has a movie come along with such a disdain for historical veracity as *Robin Hood: Prince of Thieves* (1991). We touched on some of the errors in *SON OF FILM FLUBS*, but since so many more of the film's faults have come to light, it seems to be appropriate to devote a bit more space to a wry look at things which went awry.

To reiterate, the film is set in the 1100s. But when Azeem (Morgan Freeman) uses gunpowder, he's getting the jump on Marco Polo, who not only hadn't yet brought it back with him from China, but wasn't even born until 1254 and didn't make his famous journey until 1271. In the movie, the gunpowder was being used to defend King Richard, who died in 1199.

Azeem uses a crude telescope, predating both Dutch optician Hans Lippershey, who is credited with inventing the telescope in 1608, and Galileo, who built his first one in 1609

One apparent flub in the film may well be a matter of interpretation. Many viewers noticed that when we first see Azeem in the prison, his hands are chained above his head. When Robin (Kevin Costner) escapes, Azeem's hands are down and tied together. In the dark lighting of the scene it appears that Azeem has pulled away from the wall, stood up, and twisted the chains around his hands. Your call.

There's no question of a "left to right" flub when Azeem and Robin arrive on England's shores. Robin takes a celebratory roll in the surf, and then extends his right arm to Azeem for an assist in getting up. In the next shot, we see Azeem pulling him up by his left arm. Notice also how quickly the sand disappears from Costner's face after he kisses the surf/turf.

Poor Azeem. They just didn't seem to care about the veracity of his character at all. Another history buff noticed that throughout the film he carries a curved Saracen sword; if he indeed came from the Middle East, at that time in history the broadsword would have been the weapon of choice. The Saracen scimitar came along later.

In the river fight scene with Little John (Nick Brimble), Robin gets knocked into the drink several times. But his hair seems to go from wet in the close-ups to dry when we see him in the long shots.

We're not going to delve too deeply into the language situation in *Robin Hood*. Seems like every time we get into word usage, someone comes along with differing research that proves us wrong. However, it does seem that "twit" is a word way ahead of its era, and if the infamous "f" word was indeed in existence in the twelfth century, was Will Scarlett's (Christian Slater) "Fuck me, he made it" during the catapult scene a common usage of the time? (Webster's Ninth dates it back to around 1680). And of course, Costner's accent (or lack thereof) seems to originate more in Southern California than in Northern England.

Quintessential villain Alan Rickman, as the Sheriff of Nottingham, wears a heavy-metal costume enhanced with enough studs and buckles to make Michael Jackson jealous. Michael might also be envious of the codpiece, another element which seems to be ahead of its time. An ever-so-diligent viewer went to the *Encyclopedia Brittanica*, which said that the codpiece was "worn first in the fifteenth century," and wasn't "padded, prominent, and decorated" until the sixteenth. For those who aren't familiar with ancient costumery, a codpiece was used to make the male's crotch more prominent and decorative; "stuffed pants," if you will.

And speaking of that particular area of the body geography, another sharp-eyed viewer spotted bikini brief tan lines on Costner's buns. Are we talking eleventh century Speedos?

The slipups in *Robin Hood: Prince of Thieves* are not without historical precedent. In *The Adventures of Robin Hood* (1938), Errol Flynn jumps to his horse during a rescue scene with his hands tied behind his back. In midair, Flynn's hands are in front of him, then he lands with the hands once again tied behind his back.

And in an enterprising use of existing footage, during an escape scene in *Adventures of Don Juan* (1948), Errol Flynn and Alan Hale ride from the castle. The very next scene is a chase from their earlier *Robin Hood,* with bows and arrows and an extra head bobbing along on back.

We even have what you might call a "collateral" flub, coming from *The Rocketeer* (1991). There is a sequence in that film which supposedly takes place on the set of *The Adventures of Robin Hood,* wherein you see the back of a scenery flat from the Errol Flynn–Basil Rathbone duel. The problem is that a paper coffee cup with flap handles sits on one of the flat's crossbeams. The action may be taking place in the thirties; paper cups were, as best we can tell, a fifties product.

THE FLUBS THAT COULD HAVE HAPPENED—BUT DIDN'T

A special niche in the world of flubdom has to be reserved for the ingenious filmmakers who knew that a flub was coming and managed to avoid it.

Epic director Cecil B. DeMille was a master of catching a flub aborning; in more than one instance he came up with some fascinating ways to keep the mistake from happening.

One near-miss was in *The Greatest Show on Earth* (1952). Gloria Grahame and Dorothy Lamour are in a carriage in the Marie Antoinette parade, wearing elaborate feathered headdresses. When the "dailies" came back, DeMille discovered that the film processing techniques in use at the time left a green tinge around the white feathers. So the clever DeMille inserted a shot of a light operator, high in the tent, aiming a green spotlight at the pair.

We have a group of Missouri Jesuit priests to thank for background on how DeMille was able to come up with a way to keep *King of Kings* (1927) true to biblical writ. Father William J. Federer reports that *FILM FLUBS* "entertained the Jesuit community here royally," and repays the favor by telling of the scene in *King of Kings*, wherein the woman "taken in adultery" is in the temple at Jerusalem, built for the movie as an elegant structure with a polished marbled floor. As told in the Gospel of John, Christ stooped to write on the ground as the woman was brought before him. Of course, that wouldn't have worked on the temple's marble floor.

So, to provide the dust, a girl enters carrying a bowl. She apparently hears a voice off screen summoning her, and runs away, tripping in the process. The bowl crashes to the floor, revealing that it was full of sand which spreads across the marble floor, giving Jesus a palette for his writing. An early Etch-A-Sketch, if you will. She picks up the pieces of the bowl and exits, and the scene proceeds as scripted in the Bible.

I hope the good fathers will forgive our retelling of a delightful *King of Kings* story, as related by Peter Hay in *Movie Anecdotes*. It seems that H. B. Warner, who played Jesus, took up with an extra named Sally Rand, later to become the famous "fan dancer." Rand played a slave girl to Mary Magdalene. One day, she and Warner arrived late on the set. DeMille thundered out through his megaphone: "Miss Rand, leave my Jesus Christ alone. If you must screw someone, screw Pontius Pilate!"

Softening the Way of the Cross

While we're at it, take a look at the scene in which Jeffrey Hunter as Jesus is carrying the cross in the 1961 version of *King of Kings*. He must have stopped off at the Jerusalem Plaza Mall on the way to the Via Dolorosa, because in a production still it sure looks to us like he's avoiding the pain of the cobblestones by wearing Hushpuppies. We thought sandals were the era's footwear.

Don't Fire That Guy...Reward Him!

Director Frank Capra knew when to take advantage of a flub. While filming a scene where a drunken Uncle Billy (Thomas Mitchell) staggers away in *It's a Wonderful Life* (1946), an offscreen technician bumped into a table full of props, knocking it over with a loud crash. The noise fit so well with Uncle Billy's exit that Capra left the serendipitous goof in the film and gave the guy a $10 bonus.

Incidentally, the above-mentioned H. B. Warner made a dramatic turnaround in *It's a Wonderful Life*, playing the town drunk.

Junk Food That Wasn't

Then another "flub that could have been" involves Meryl Streep's snack food in *Postcards From the Edge* (1990). Streep's character is a junk-food addict, going through bag after bag of Fritos Corn Chips. But several folks noticed that the chips she pulls out aren't Fritos. Nope, they're health food chips, which Streep asked propmaster C. J. Maguire to put in the bags.

65

MEET THE CREW

There's a perverse delight in spotting someone who really shouldn't be in a scene. From time to time, it's a casual spectator, as in *Bullitt* (1968) when, while Steve McQueen is talking to a couple of ladies in a restaurant, a man comes walking by in the background. A security guard pops into the scene and pulls him away.

More often than not, we get a brief glimpse of an actual crew member. It may be someone operating a camera which is simultaneously shooting from another direction, as in *The Fabulous Baker Boys* (1989) when the brothers Bridges fight in an alley after a bogus telethon. As the two go flying into a wire fence, you can see a man with a hand-held camera jump out of the way.

Occasionally, you'll get an inadvertent look at a crew member in a reflection in a mirror or some shiny surface. The former can be found in *Sleuth* (1972). There are supposed to be only two characters in the film, but when Laurence Olivier opens a window, you can see the reflection of a stagehand. The shiny chrome around a car mirror reveals the camera crew in Clint Eastwood's *Pink Cadillac* (1989).

More unintentional introductions:

Excuse Me, Miss…

About halfway through *Compromising Positions* (1985), when she and Judith Ivey (the "cuppycake" lady) are riding in a car, Susan Sarandon gets a dialogue cue when a finger comes from the back seat and taps her on the shoulder.

Sticking It to the Bear

A bear crashes through a door, which falls atop John Candy in *The Great Outdoors* (1988). As the bear bounces on the door, the trainer's yellow stick can be seen poking at it.

A Helping Hand for the Batmobile

When Michael Keaton calls for the Batmobile in *Batman* (1989), the car supposedly starts up by itself and drives up an alley. As John McLaughlin would say on TV, "Wrong!" In one of the front shots, a hand can be seen on the steering wheel.

A Gigi Giggle

In *Gigi* (1958), when a woman gets out of bed and crosses to screen right, you see the mirror reflection of a crew member holding a cable.

Down at the Station, Early in the Morning, See the Camera Crew

As Devereaux (Patrick McGoohan) burns the Rembrandt letters in his compartment in *Silver Streak* (1976), the train begins to pull out of the station. As you'd expect, the station seems to move away as the train moves. But instead of the train itself being reflected in the station's windows, you see a handcar containing a camera crew—filming the rear-screen projection that you're *really* seeing.

News Crews, Real and Otherwise

As the McKims (John Gregson and Dinah Sheridan) drive up to the (real) BBC man Leslie Matthews, the crew can be seen as shadows in the bottom of the frame in *Genevieve* (1953).

Shadow of the Light Man

As Nick Charles (William Powell) is playing with Asta, the dog, in the locker room at the race track in *Shadow of the Thin Man* (1941), look for a man reflected in a pane of glass lighting the scene.

The Not-So-Hidden Camera

When the characters in *Sweet Heart's Dance* (1988) go on a tropical vacation, there's a scene on a hotel balcony where you can see another camera crew, shooting the reverses, facing directly toward the camera that's filming the action.

A Hairy Moment

Elizabeth Taylor is supposedly alone in the room when she stands in front of a mirror in *Butterfield 8* (1960). But you can briefly see a crew member's hairy arm in the mirror.

More Than One Debut

Bad Boys (1983) starred Sean Penn and was Ally Sheedy's screen debut. But was it also the cameraman's screen debut? Look for him in the fight sequence at the end of the movie, standing with a hand-held camera in the group of kids that circle the action.

Along for the Ride

In the final scene of *The Road Warrior* (1981), Mel Gibson is driving a tanker, and everyone is wearing post-holocaust attire—except in an interior shot, where a cameraman in 1980s garb films the getaway.

Not So Alone in the Woods

Albert Popwell stops his car in a wooded area where Clint Eastwood as Dirty Harry is shooting at a silhouette target in *Sudden Impulse* (1983). The two are supposedly alone in the woods—except for the cameraman, whom you can see in a quick reflection in the car's vent window.

Wandering Past Its Own Reflection

As the camera wanders around Sean Connery's apartment building in *The Untouchables* (1987), it not only catches the action—it catches itself. Both the crane and crew can be seen in a reflection in a window.

Was the Crew Dancing, Too?

In *Xanadu* (1980), during Olivia Newton-John and Gene Kelly's song and dance number, "Whenever You're Away From Me," there's a moment when the vocals have stopped and they're dancing to the music. As they go past a large mirror you can see the film crew.

Rats! They Saw Me!

As Bruce Davison is mixing Ben the rat's food with poison in the kitchen in *Willard* (1981), you can see a trainer who is putting Willard on his mark reflected in one of the glass doors.

71

The Not-So-Secret Hiding Place

As Pee-wee Herman (a.k.a. Paul Reubens) waters the lawn near the beginning of *Pee-wee's Big Adventure* (1985), he enters a secret code to access his bike's hiding place. A door opens, and if you'll look closely at the left side of the garage, a leg moves quickly out of the shot.

Wizardry They Didn't Count On

The shiny silver helmet that Nicol Williamson wears as the wizard Merlin in *Excalibur* (1981) performs a bit of wizardry on its own, showing us the cameraman in a scene near the end of the film.

Falling in Love With a Reflection

The camera can be seen in a mirror in the Meryl Streep–Robert De Niro romance *Falling in Love* (1984).

PROP PROBLEMS

Props can be both the *bête noire* of the filmmaker and a treasure trove for an alert flub-spotter. The term "props" (originally "properties") covers a wide range of items, from the physical things that an actor carries into a scene ("hand props," such as guns and knives) to bottles and glasses and the little gewgaws and tschatschkes ("set dressing") that add atmosphere and verisimilitude to the set.

Since most props aren't nailed down, there's always a chance that they can make an inadvertent move between one shot and another, causing a "jump" on the screen; they can be overlooked when the set is re-dressed from one scene to another, thus disappearing in the next shot; or something can happen from shot to shot that creates a noticeable change, such as the level of liquid in a bottle coming and going. They can even be the source of anachronisms, when the set decorator isn't watching his p's and q's.

Such was the case in *Mommie Dearest* (1981) when little Tina Crawford is at the bar, fixing a drink for one of her "uncles." On a counter can be seen a bottle of "Fantastik" cleaner, a product that certainly wasn't around in the late forties, the era of that particular scene. Prop problem.

In the controversial *Basic Instinct* (1992), as Michael Douglas and George Dzundza talk in a diner, the cap from a ketchup bottle is dropped and rattles onto the table. Next shot, it's back on the bottle again, even though neither of the two retrieved it. But someone on the prop crew must have fixed it between the two shots. Prop problem.

The World's Fastest Purse-Snatcher

Just before Teri Garr knocks on Dustin Hoffman's door in *Tootsie* (1982), Hoffman's purse is laying on a table. In the next shot, it's gone. Now, is that a fast purse-snatcher, or what?

Maybe the Same Crook Stole 'Em Both

After she leaves the nursing home and goes back to the Whistle Stop Cafe in *Fried Green Tomatoes* (1991), Jessica Tandy is seen sitting on her suitcase as she wonders who "stole" her house. She might also ponder who slipped in and then stole her suitcase. An alert flub-spotter noticed that neither she nor Kathy Bates seems to be carrying it when they go back to the car, nor is it still in the road.

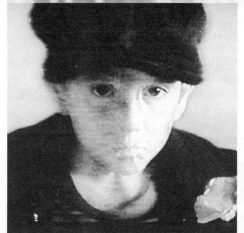

Another Glass of Milk, Please

When Dick Tracy and Tess Trueheart are in the diner with The Kid in *Dick Tracy* (1990), The Kid finishes a glass of milk, then runs for the door. Tracy puts him back in his seat, during which time the glass has magically refilled itself.

Maybe It Was Just a Very Wealthy Tribe

Near the end of *Outrageous Fortune* (1987), a handful of money is thrown from a cliff, to be gathered up by a tribe of Indians. But there are those who couldn't wait. If you look closely, before the dough is tossed, some of the Indians already have wads of the prop money stuffed in their pockets.

75

Thelma's Magical Margarita

While *Dick Tracy*'s "kid" (Charlie Korsmo) is having trouble with that glass of milk, the same thing happens in a less wholesome situation in *Thelma and Louise* (1991). In the country-western bar scene, while Geena Davis dances, Susan Sarandon finds the magical margarita. For most of the scene, when we see her from the front taking a drink, it's down about an inch. But in the shots over her shoulder, it's full to the brim.

Liver, When You're Near Me...

Maybe Kevin Costner just didn't have the gumption to take a big bite out of that buffalo liver in *Dances With Wolves* (1990). In the long shots, it looks rather large, but in the close-ups, it's not only smaller but of a different shape. Did the prop people create something a bit more palatable for Costner between shots?

Calling Father Flanagan

In the 1986 TV movie, *Miracle of the Heart: A Boystown* [sic] *Story*, with Art Carney and Casey Siemaszko updating the old Spencer Tracy and Mickey Rooney roles, the producers had a heck of a time getting things straight, leaving the prop department to its own devices. The title had the famed locale incorrectly designated as a single word, while the T-shirts worn by the young delinquents spelled it "Boy's Town" (also incorrectly with an apostrophe). At least the road signs outside the camp had it right—as Boys Town.

The Wreath That Wouldn't Go Away

One of Leonard Maltin's discoveries as revealed on "Entertainment Tonight" is Jimmy Stewart's problem with a wreath in *It's a Wonderful Life* (1946). He comes into the newspaper office carrying a wreath on his arm and tosses it casually aside, and picks up the phone. In the next shot, the wreath has popped back onto his arm.

Outreach and Touch Someone

We're not so sure that the prop makers and the set crew were communicating on *Scrooged* (1988). Karen Allen hands Bill Murray her business card, which reads "Operation Reachout." But when Murray calls on her at work, the sign on the building reads "Operation Outreach."

TV or Not TV, That Is the Question

We have to think about this one a bit. In *The Girl Can't Help It* (1956), Jayne Mansfield and Tom Ewell return to her townhouse and receive a frantic phone call from Jayne's mobster boyfriend (Edmond O'Brien), telling her to turn on the TV set to a certain channel. She does, and we see a color picture. In the 1950s color TV's were a rarity. We have to assume that a piece of color film was rear-projected onto a fake TV on the set. Let this serve as a warning to the colorizers when they see a TV picture in an old black-and-white movie! Touch not that screen.

Batman Can't Spell

Batman (1989) had more than its share of prop spelling problems, as detailed in *FILM FLUBS*. Yet another has been unearthed: On the menus next to the tables in the museum restaurant, the spelling is "Fluegelheim Museum." On a sign, an "e" is lost and it becomes "Flugelheim Museum."

Ask Not for Whom the Anvil Tolls

Yet another flub spotter who watched the filming of *Glory* (1989) in Savannah reveals director Edward Zwick's ingenious solution when confronted with background noise. It seems that a new bridge was being built over the Savannah River not far away, and a pile driver was making a prodigious noise. Directors have, of course, all kinds of power, but stopping construction on a bridge project might just be outside the realm of possibility. So Zwick put a blacksmith in the background, hitting an anvil in perfect time with each strike of the pile driver.

The Prince of Tides

Before we get into it, there's something about this film we just have to discuss. What with all the controversy about Streisand's directing—which is, we have to admit, not bad—and the Oscar "snub," why would a director set up so many shots where the focus is on her star's (in this case, herself) glamorous manicure rather than on the scene itself? The constant display of nails is distracting, and we wonder if someone else had directed, would the show of hands been permitted?

We were also a bit troubled with Barbra's hands in one of the scenes in her office. As she sits on the front edge of her desk while talking to Nick Nolte, it seems that her hands make some awfully fast moves from her lap to the desk behind her.

The ever-so-sharp-eyed readers of *Premiere* magazine reported to our friend Rob Medich of the "Gaffe Squad" that when Nolte arrives at his sister's apartment in New York, he's in a Yellow Cab with the medallion number 6X24. Days later, he escorts Streisand's real-to-reel son, Jason Gould, to Grand Central Station, and the cab which takes them there once more is 6X24. And when Nolte and Streisand leave the disastrous dinner party, there's good old 6X24 waiting for them again. How's that for a cinematic coincidence, given that there are 11,787 licensed cabs in New York City?

When Susan Lowenstein (Streisand) takes Tom Wingo (Nolte) to her country home, they arrive laden with groceries. As they enter the house for the first time, almost all the doors and windows are open. Is it safe to leave your unoccupied place open in that part of the country?

You might also notice that while Nolte waits for Streisand across the street from her office building, there's a rather busy extra. A man in a light suit with shoulder-length blond hair passes behind him, right to left. Then, in a close-up, there he comes again, right to left.

KNOWING YOUR LEFT FROM YOUR RIGHT

In the making of a film, several factors can cause things to be switched mistakenly from left to right. The most obvious factor, is, of course, carelessness. When one take ends and another begins, someone on the set may fail to notice that something has moved. An actor who, in the original take, might have been sitting or standing, may move to a different position, or might hold a prop in a different hand.

Another is "screen direction." To keep from jarring the eye of the viewer, the movement on screen has to have a certain continuous direction. Imagine that you're seeing a train come into the picture from upper left, crossing the picture diagonally to lower right. If, in the cut to another shot of the train, the movement is from right to left, it's a visual disturbance, a disorienting moment that catches your attention. Like-wise, if a character is looking to the right when talking in one shot, then looks to the left when listening to another actor's response, it catches your attention and creates as visually confusing moment. And if an actor who is walking down the street goes off screen to the right, he'd better come back on from the left or you'll think he turned around.

Another visual principle that operates in this kind of situation is that the camera can't "cross the line" in a particular scene. A convention of single-camera filming is that there's an imaginary line between the noses of two people as they face each other in a single shot. This gives the camera a 180° range of movement during a shot. As long as the camera stays on the same side of the "line" during a scene, the shots will cut into each other with no problem. Should it cross the barrier to the other side, the editor has one hell of a time making things look right on screen.

Which is not to say that there aren't some tricks of the trade to cover one's behind if things go wrong. One time-honored method for editors to use if there's a shot-to-shot mismatch or a problem in screen direction is to intercut a "neutral" shot between two takes. Say, for example, an actor's cigarette dramatically changes length from take to take. The editor inserts a shot in between the two to reduce the effect. She might well go from a shot of the actor smoking a short cigarette to a shot of the dinner table then back to the actor with a longer cigarette. Most people, hopefully, won't notice the mismatch.

Of course, even that technique didn't work too well in *City Slickers* (1991). As Jack Palance and Billy Crystal ride along side by side, notice Palance's cigarette as it goes from short to long and several lengths in between.

Another way to solve a problem in screen direction or a line cross is to flip the film. This is really dangerous ground. The image on the film has to be relatively clean of offending objects to prevent signs from being reversed or movement of recognizable objects to the wrong side. For example, there's the "speedboat" scene in *Indiana Jones and the Last Crusade* (1989), just after one of the power boats is chewed up by a larger craft's propellers. All along, Indy's girlfriend has been steering the powerboat from the right side. But in a long shot, she and the steering wheel suddenly switch to the left. It appears that the film was flipped to maintain screen direction...and perhaps they hoped we wouldn't notice that the steering wheel moved over. Sorry. We caught it.

Physician, Reverse Thyself

Acting out the "physician, heal thyself" adage, pounced-upon medical student Kiefer Sutherland stitches up a gash on his own right cheek in *Flatliners* (1990). In the next shot, the scar is gone, then it reappears on his left cheek, where it remains for the rest of the film.

Left Side Story

As Victoria Tennant's car starts to roll away in *L.A. Story* (1991), she climbs in on the driver's side and Steve Martin on the passenger side. Yet a few minutes later when they get out at the talking highway sign, he emerges from the driver's side. Did they stop and change seats?

At Least They're in the Same Bed

Joanne Woodward's performance in *Mr. and Mrs. Bridge* (1990) is truly a wonder—a tour-de-force in seamless acting technique. But you have to wonder why while she and real-life hubby Paul Newman are in bed in the hotel in Paris, they switch sides and then switch back again. It couldn't be unbridled passion; both Mr. and Mrs. are too cool and reserved for that. At least they're in the same bed; in the old days, the Hays Office would have insisted on twin beds. And in the sequence when Paul Newman is having beer in the kitchen, isn't that a modern Budweiser label on the bottle in a scene set in the early thirties?

A Reversal of Bread

Claus von Bülow (Jeremy Irons), in *Reversal of Fortune* (1990), hires lawyer Alan Dershowitz (Ron Silver), and they "take a meeting" at a restaurant. Irons has a piece of bread close to his mouth, about to take a bite. In the next shot, the bread is in the same position, but he has switched hands. Silver, however, is cool to the situation. In fact, during the meal when a lemon he squeezes squirts him in the face, he holds character and doesn't react at all.

The Eye-Crossing Injury

Tom Cruise is hurt in a racetrack crash and is taken to the hospital in *Days of Thunder* (1990). His right eye is injured and you see a red ring around it. But a few scenes later, the injury has moved to his left eye.

Left Hook or Right: Either Way, an Interesting Maneuver

The traditional Captain Hook in Barrie's *Peter Pan* had a missing right hand; however, word is that Dustin Hoffman had trouble using his left hand as the operating one, so in *Hook* (1991) his left one bears the hook. This makes for an interesting situation after the invasion of Wendy's home. If a left-hooked Captain made the deep scratch up the right wall of the stairwell, then he had to either go up backward or do an intricate cross-chest maneuver to scar the right-hand wall.

At least we don't have to worry about the original Captain Hook's right hand. Word is that it found work in *The Addams Family* as "Thing."

A Flipped-Out Deer Hunter

It appears that some film was flipped in *The Deer Hunter* (1978). When Robert De Niro goes on a hunting trip, he stalks a deer in the high mountains of the Appalachians. Watch as both the bolt on his rifle and his wristwatch change sides several times. And by the way, although the scene is set in North Carolina, folks in the Northwest recognized it as Washington's Mount Baker, a 10,778-foot-high Northern Cascades behemoth. North Carolina's Mount Mitchell tops out around 6,600 feet.

Countering the Move (or Moving at the Counter)

Peter Falk and a cab driver change sides in the cutaways as they sit at a bar in *The In-Laws* (1979).

Cheeky Changeover

A dog comes over and licks Ariel's cheek as she looks over the side of the Prince's boat in *The Little Mermaid* (1989). The dog licks her right side, but she rubs her left cheek.

Cheeky Changeover II: We're Not Out of the Woods Yet

In *First Blood* (1982), a.k.a. *Rambo I*, sheriff Brian Dennehy follows Rambo (Sylvester Stallone) into the woods. Rambo surprises him pushing the sheriff up against the tree and cutting his left cheek. However, throughout the rest of the film, the cut is on his right cheek.

Did Raquel Teach the Child Left From Right?

A solicitous Tawnee Welch massages Steve Guttenberg's right leg just after he bangs it in *Cocoon* (1985). As they talk, mysteriously the left leg becomes the injured one.

Taking New Sides

At the beginning of *I Remember Mama* (1948), the "aunts" Jenny (on the right) and Sigrid (left) sit at a table drinking coffee. When Jenny asks "Where are the children?" and gets up, she and Aunt Sigrid have changed places.

Round and Round the Ferris Wheel Goes...

We have this one straight from the horse's mouth, as it were. Watch the scene at the amusement park on the pier in Steven Spielberg's *1941* (1979), and you'll see the riflemen sitting side by side on the ferris wheel swap seats as it goes around. Not only was this gaffe noticed by several erstwhile flub-spotters, but they were even alerted to it by one of the two actors who made the switch, thereby earning for himself special laurels in the Flubbie Hall of Fame.

The Surreal Thing

John Goodman, as Charlie Meadows, complains of an ear infection in *Barton Fink* (1991) and wears cotton in his right ear. But when he returns from one of his mysterious trips late in the film, he treats the infection in his left ear. Did it spread to the other side, or was it just one more of the strange aspects of the film, such as the disappearance of the bodies of the detectives after they are gunned down in the hallway? Of course, by that time surrealism has crept into the production, so just about any explanation will probably suffice.

COSTUME CHANGES

The glitches that bedevil the wardrobe supervisors seem to be changes, more often than not, that happen in front of the cameras, rather than in costume design and preparation—even though zippers and other modern devices occasionally show up in period costumes.

Of course, the director and script supervisor should catch these little gremlins either at the time they happen or when the "dailies" are checked. But moviemakers are only human, and things slip by.

I compare it to the purchase of a new car. Have you ever bought a car that didn't have some little thing wrong with it, whether it's a missing trim screw or a door that doesn't shut right? You can always take it back to the dealer for a fix. But cars are assembly-line products, each pretty much like the ones that went before it. Every movie, whether a spectacle or a made-for-video "B" potboiler, is a unique product, and in the making of it there can be little mistakes and oversights. Just look at the list of names in the end credits. Every one of those people had something to do with the creation of that product—the movie you're watching. It's surprising that there aren't more mistakes, and that any film can make it to the screen sans a gaffe or two.

But they happen, and we catch 'em. We offer as testimony:

He Knocked the Polka Dots Right Off His Tie

Humphrey Bogart backhands Peter Lorre in *The Maltese Falcon* (1941). When Lorre's head snaps left, he's wearing a polka-dot bow tie. When it snaps back to the right, he's wearing a striped one.

The Little Tramp and His Wandering Hat

Charlie Chaplin couldn't keep up with his trademark hat in *The Vagabond* (1916). When the Little Tramp is being chased around and through a bar, he falls and loses his hat outside the place but when he enters again he's wearing it. He then exits once more, hatless, and outside picks up the hat off the sidewalk where he originally dropped it.

Charlie's hat problems continue when he rescues a gypsy girl, and her father tries to drown him in a washtub. He escapes soaking wet and hatless, and jumps onto the back of a wagon, spitting water in the father's face. In the next shot, he's climbing into the front of the wagon, not only wearing the hat, but bone dry.

Unexpected Modesty

There's not an excess of modesty in the porn business, as explored in *Hardcore* (1979), but shortly after she's seen totally nude in a peep booth, Season Hubley's panties appear.

Unexpected Modesty II: The Adventure Continues

Another bit of undergarment prestidigitation takes place in *National Lampoon's Animal House* (1978) when Tim Matheson is kissing and fondling a girl in a car. As he lifts her top off it's clear that she is wearing no bra. When his pals come out of the Dexter Lake Club, she screams and jumps out, wearing nothing but her skirt and shoes. But when she lands in the car next to her, a bra has magically appeared.

It's Better to Be Safe Than Sexy

Things may not be as steamy on the set as they appear in many movies. Take *Sea of Love* (1989), for example. Al Pacino meets up with Ellen Barkin, and soon they're in bed for a bit of horizontal recreation. Afterward, as Pacino sits on the edge of the bed to pull on his underwear, you can see the tops of the briefs he's already wearing. Two pair?

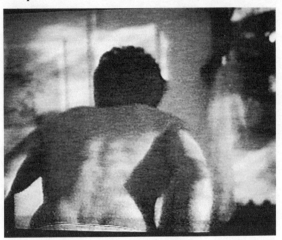

Damn the Continuity, Full Speed Ahead

Director Leo McCarey always cut for the funniest takes in a Marx Brothers movie, continuity be damned. Thus in *Duck Soup* (1933), in the opening reception for Rufus J. Firefly, Groucho's coat changes from gray with braids to tails and back again.

The Countess—Now Two Inches Shorter

Sophia Loren and Marlon Brando are in his stateroom on the ship in *A Countess From Hong Kong* (1967). Director Charlie Chaplin didn't notice that she started the scene wearing high heels and walked away at the end in flats.

Fallen on the Battlefield

Somebody caught it and fixed it, but not soon enough for one of Michael Lerner's military medals to create a very obvious flub in *Barton Fink* (1991). As Lerner, playing movie mogul Jack Lipnick, argues with John Turturro, in the title role, one of his campaign ribbons slips and dangles lopsidedly on its pin. In the next shot, it's neatly back in place.

God Help the Script Girl

The Beatles wear different clothing from one shot to another in the opening dash-onto-the-train sequence of *A Hard Day's Night* (1964). The "why" of the moment has been preserved for posterity by continuity supervisor Rita Davison. Her notes for the shot, as quoted by Peter Van Gelder in *That's Hollywood*, say: "First shot taken while I was in the ladies' toilet. I think they were the Beatles, but they were wearing the clothing which they came in with, and not what was supposed to be worn. It was photographed by the director. I trust this is not the way we intend to go on. God help me."

The Leaky Space Suit

Dave Bowen's space suit isn't very airtight in a shot in *2001: A Space Odyssey* (1968). When he reenters the Discovery spaceship with its atmosphere evacuated, he opens an access hatch to the HAL 9000 logic center and climbs over the camera into the chamber wearing his E.V.A. airtight space suit. As his left hand moves past, the glove separates from the sleeve, showing his bare wrist.

And hey, you want to have a little fun? Think about the name of the computer: HAL. Then think about the letter that follows each in the alphabet. Arthur Clarke said it was just a coincidence.

OOPSIES

Some flubs defy explanation. They're usually just little slipups, things that nobody noticed on the set. By the time these oopsies make it to the final film, it's just too late to do anything about them.

Perhaps it's a little problem with a prop—such as in the controversial *Basic Instinct* (1992), where on the door plate of her office, the psychologist's name is spelled "Elisabeth Garner"; but when Michael Douglas pulls her name up on a computer, it's "Elizabeth Garner."

Then there's *Chicago Joe and the Showgirl* (1990), a British film. Remember that. British. The movie is set in London of the 1940s, and when Kiefer Sutherland is arrested by a Bobby, his rights are read to him. But the Miranda law didn't come about until the 1970s. Then again, why were they reading him his rights? Miranda is an *American* law.

More slips and slides:

Nothing Ever Is As You See It

Joan Blondell, turning up as Vi, the waitress in *Grease* (1978), consoles one of the students, who tells her, "Beauty school isn't what I thought it would be." Vi responds, "Nothing ever is," and heads into the kitchen with a tray of dishes. On the way in, she tries to flip off the light switch with her elbow and misses it by a country mile. The switch stays in the "on" position, but the lights go off anyway.

Going Off With the Bushes...But Not George and Barbara

You usually don't see too many flubs in animation, it being a meticulous, detailed art. But they do happen—as in Disney masterpiece *Fantasia* (1940). Notice that during the Pastoral Symphony sequence, when a pair of centaurs go off to woo, a bush at the bottom right corner of the screen goes along with them.

Take a Seat, Please

During the "Grant Avenue" musical number in *Flower Drum Song* (1961), dancers on the front row kick their feet forward and down on one hand, except for one who lands on her tushie.

Rodney Takes a Hairy Dive

Rodney Dangerfield takes a dive in *Back to School* (1986)—a "triple Lindy" from the high board. Look closely, and you'll see that it's Rodney starting the dive, but on the way down it's a double whose toupee flaps up to reveal his bald pate.

Anything to Help Out

When one of the hit men in the zany comedy *A Weekend at Bernie's* (1989) was knocked cold and dragged into a closet, he conveniently lifts his feet so the closet door can shut. Since a sequel is scheduled for 1992, wonder if they might appropriate the title *Dead Again?*

Yet Another *JFK* Conspiracy

We've said it before—if you have a piece of equipment in a shot, you'd better know how to run it. If it's not right, someone will always notice. A professional cameraman who works for Twentieth Century Fox was so bothered by a technical oversight in *JFK* (1991) that he wrote to tell us about it.

Seems that in one of the shots, a 16mm Mitchell camera (one that was often used for news coverage before the advent of video Betacams) is filming a speech. Our astute camera operator noticed that while the take-up reel is working, the feed reel is still. That would indicate that there is no film in the camera, since under normal circumstances one would pull the other and both would be rolling.

Sorta reminiscent of the reporter's empty cassette recorder in *Presumed Innocent* (1990), isn't it?

A Bit Too Flirtatious

One more, and we're off the subject (how's that for a double entendre?). In *Grease* (1978), when Dinah Manoff, playing Marty Maraschino, flirts with Edd "Kookie" Byrnes with the TV camera in the background, just after she says "Maraschino, like in cherries" her strapless dress slips, exposing a generous amount of breast. She quickly covers it with her dance card, but for a frame or two you can see her look of surprise. Kookie is out of frame at the moment, but we'd love to see the look on his face!

2A or Not 2D

In *Soap Dish* (1991), when Sally Field asks the doorman the number of Kevin Kline's apartment, she is told "2D." But later, when she leaves, the number on the door is "2A."

Producer Alan Greisman admitted to an interviewer that it was an error caused by writing down the wrong numbers when the prop people went to buy them. It was noticed in edit and an attempt was made to re-record the doorman's lines to "2A," but this looked so awkward that the decision was made to leave in the gaffe.

No Call for the Cops

When Warner Bros. needed a new movie for its star dog Rin Tin Tin, the studio sometimes came up with the title before the script was written. Thus *Tracked by the Police* (1927) actually has Rin Tin Tin as the tracker—and no police anywhere in the film.

Shanghai'd From Shanghai

Exiled to Shanghai (1937) was not about anyone being exiled, and the story didn't take place in Shanghai. Then, in a case of film history repeating itself, no character, either male or female, is from Shanghai in *The Lady From Shanghai* (1948), Orson Welles's film that contains his famous Hall of Mirrors sequence. Welles said that he dreamed up the title to coax production money from studio boss Harry Cohn.

Best Breast Forward

Watch for this one on a late movie or one of the movie classics channels, since it isn't out on home video yet. In *Susan Hayward: Portrait of a Survivor*, a 1960 biography by Beverly Linet, Robert Wagner is quoted as saying that after hearing that a theater owner had spotted a delightful flub in *With a Song in My Heart* (1952), he couldn't find it. But never doubt the abilities of a dedicated flub-spotter. Martha Heneger says she found it in the title song number, about fifty-seven minutes into the film. The flub? Susan Hayward's strapless evening dress slips, exposing her left breast.

But Hayward wasn't the first to inadvertently be exposed on film. For a brief, one- or two-frame moment, when Fay Wray surfaces in the water in *King Kong* (1933), her dress slips and you glimpse a bit more of her decolletàge than either she or director Merian C. Cooper intended. And in *Red Headed Woman* (1932), a film that was made before the Hays Office did its dirty work, Jean Harlow briefly displays a breast.

Privates Practice

A tickled and titillated viewer reports that in an episode of TV's *St. Elsewhere* wherein the doctors are in a steam bath, all are draped in towels. But when Dr. Morrison (David Morse) stands up, you get a quick glimpse of all his privates.

Wagner's Wingwang Wigwags

We'll take someone else's word for this one: in *All the Fine Young Cannibals* (1960), a film which we hear is so bad that one really just can't sit through it, Robert Wagner's wingwang can be seen to visibly wigwag through the fabric of his trousers. You go look. We don't wanna.

A Ruse by Any Other Name

What does a studio do when it has the misfortune of releasing a picture with the term "Communist" in the title just as Senator Joseph McCarthy was making it a truly dirty word? RKO simply changed the title of *I Married a Communist* (1950) to *Woman on Pier 13* in mid-run (in some locations it showed with one title, in others with a new one). Some filmgoers thought they were going to see a patriotic potboiler, while others presumed they would be viewing a "lady in distress" flick.

BACK FROM THE DEAD

Playing a dead body in an extended scene has to be a real challenge for an actor. After all, one does have to breathe from time to time. And blink. It's one of those involuntary reflex reactions to light, dust, or dryness which is very hard to control.

In the days of live television it was really a problem. There are several stories about "dead" actors getting up and walking off the set, not realizing that the camera was still on them. Movies, however, are another matter. The camera can be stopped to let the dead respirate. Even so, they can slip up.

Actors can experience a resurrection in other ways, too. Sometimes it's a matter of their being in a scene which becomes part of the story long after they've "died"—more often than not a result of nonsequential shooting.

Examples:

Depends on Your View of Reality

During one scene in *Total Recall* (1990), a psychiatrist is sent in to convince Arnold Schwarzenegger's character that everything going on is a dream. He says that he has been injected into the dream to bring him back to reality. Arnie responds by killing the doctor with a shot to the head. But later, when Schwarzenegger is being strapped down for reprogramming, the "dead" doctor is moving around in the background.

The Dead Can Be Startled, Too

When divers enter the sunken submarine in *The Abyss* (1989), they are startled when they open a hatchway and a crewman's body comes floating toward them. The late crewman must have been a bit startled, too. Look closely and you'll see him blink when the bright light hits his face.

Feeling Good About Being Dead

Maybe we'd better think twice about Dan Aykroyd's mortuary in *My Girl* (1991). Are these people really dead, or is this a replay of *Murders in the Rue Morgue*? The body of the old schoolmarm appears to be breathing, as does that of young Thomas J. (Macauley Culkin).

Our flub-spotters are unforgiving. Someone noticed that when Thomas J.'s mother turns over Vada's (Anna Chlumsky) mood ring, which Thomas J. was holding, it's a bright turquoise, usually indicating that you feel pretty good. Remember mood rings? When they weren't worn in a while, away from body heat, they turned a motley blue/black.

Was It Involuntary Muscular Reactions?

When Robin Williams and the Lost Boys are fighting the pirates in *Hook* (1991), they kill a few, who move around after they're dead.

Dilating the Truth

We hate to break the illusion, but there are a couple of flaws in one of the greatest death scenes ever—Janet Leigh's departure in *Psycho* (1960). For one thing, she swallows after being dead. Neat trick. Then there's that extreme close-up of her eye. Notice that the pupil is contracted to a pinpoint, an obvious reaction to the bright lighting on the set.

When the movie was first released, director Alfred Hitchcock received letters from quite a few ophthalmologists, pointing out that when you're dead, your pupils dilate. They suggested that the effect could be created with belladonna eyedrops, which he used on the "dead" in later films.

103

Guttenberg's Movable Eyes

A young Steve Guttenberg, on the trail of Nazi-in-hiding Josef Mengele (Gregory Peck) in *The Boys From Brazil* (1978), is stabbed by Mengele's henchmen. He slumps to the floor with his back to the wall, supposedly dead. After which he blinks several times.

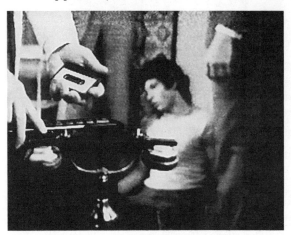 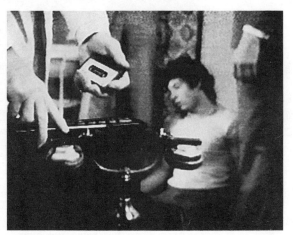

Just Keeping Up With What Was Going on in the Room

A dead man hangs from a coat hook behind a door in *Silent Rage* (1982), but as the door is slowly opened, the corpse's eyes move. When it's closed, they move again.

Politicians Never Die

The Vietnam vet holds a dead politician against a garbage truck in the Charlie Sheen–Emilio Estevez family epic, *Men At Work* (1991), while trying to convince the police officer that everything is okay. The corpse does its part; it blinks.

Alan Rickman Scares Me, Too

Bruce Willis sends a dead terrorist down the elevator shaft in *Die Hard* (1988). Dastardly Alan Rickman turns him over, and just as Rickman's hand nears his face, the startled corpse blinks.

The Addams Family

In the evolutionary process from cartoon to cult-favorite TV series to big-screen movie, it's a shame that *The Addams Family* lost its *raison d'être*. It just wasn't funny. But enough people liked it to turn it into a hit, thus opening the doors to us for a few hits at its flubs.

Speaking of doors, that's where we first turn our attention. Notice that there are two "ejection chute" doors on the side of the house. At first viewing, the door on the left bears Pugsley's name, the one on the right Wednesday's. That's the way we see them when Uncle Fester is expelled. A little later, Wednesday escapes via her door, but this time it's on the left. Then, a few minutes later, when the family searches for her, the names are back in their original positions.

In one sequence, Gomez pulls the chain that sends Uncle Fester and him down the corkscrew slide to the lower vaults. As they slide they change places a couple of times, even though it seems too narrow for them to switch.

Note also that Margaret has some problems with the finger trap. First, she wears it, then is seen not wearing it—indicating that she must have known how to take it off. Then she puts it back on, but can't get it off until Morticia shows her how the next day.

Outside a motel, Lurch drinks some "lemonade" which makes him blow fire out of his mouth—burning the paint off a nearby wooden Indian and leaving it blackened, but in the next scene, it has been wondrously healed, paint and all.

At the party near the end of the film, Gomez juggles some rather dangerous objects. When the camera is on his face—and not showing the juggling—he smiles broadly as though he's having a very good time. Yet in the angled overhead shot, you see a very stern stunt double concentrating very hard on his performance.

JEWELRY THEFTS AND RELATED ADVENTURES

Jewelry—it's a real shot-to-shot problem. It can move, it can appear, it can disappear. It can even change shape and form. It can be, you should pardon our glee, a wonderful place from which to mine a few flubs.

One of our favorite comes from *Superman* (1978). Krypton is, of course, a mythical planet, one from which Marlon Brando as Jor-El dispatches his young son into outer space as destruction nears. We wonder if Brando had been on a scouting trip to Earth in some earlier adventure— a trip in which he acquired a Rolex wristwatch. There's a brief glimpse of it on his wrist as he puts the baby into the space capsule.

An interesting little flub happens in *Father of the Bride* (1991). Someone who knows about such things noticed that Diane Keaton's rings were reversed. She wore her engagement ring closest to her palm, while traditionally the wedding band is worn in that position ("closest to the heart").

While we're on the subject of wedding rings, we've heard from several would-be flub spotters who noticed nuns wearing wedding rings in various movies. That's not a flub. Most nuns wear wedding bands to symbolize their vows to be "a bride of Christ." It would probably be a flub if an actress playing a nun did *not* wear a band.

A Rank Problem

In the opening scenes of *Glory* (1989), Matthew Broderick says how proud he is to have been made captain. He has two bars on his shoulders, indicating that rank. But in the next shot they're gone, dropping him back to second lieutenant. Still later the bars are back again.

And we just can't leave *Glory* alone. Well, when a movie is this fine, it's even more fun to find its cinema slipups. A favorite in this corner: As his regiment marches through a Southern town, Morgan Freeman stops to talk to some children. When he leaves to rejoin his regiment, they wave to him, but as they raise their hands, notice that the youngest on the far right is wearing a digital watch.

One more and we're through: When the regiment goes into battle for the first time, notice that in one shot their rifles have no bayonets, in another they do, then they're gone again, but back again later during hand-to-hand combat.

The Perils of Pearls

When going to visit Jessica Tandy at the nursing home for what turns out to be the last time in *Fried Green Tomatoes* (1991), Kathy Bates is wearing an off-white dress and a strand of pearls. In the next shot, the pearls are gone; they're back again when she arrives in the hospital room, then they vanish once more.

Make a Good Impression—And Save a Few Bucks

Michael Douglas does a nice sleight of hand in *Romancing the Stone* (1984) showing that his character is pretty cheap. He takes a very elaborate necklace out of his pocket and hands it to Kathleen Turner. But when she takes it, it's a simple charm on a chain.

Did Anyone Videotape It?

Demi Moore and Rob Lowe are making out in a jeep in *St. Elmo's Fire* (1985) when things get so hot that her long dangling earrings come and go several times.

Did Anyone Videotape It?: II

Andie McDowell wears a necklace when she's sitting in a chair and asking her husband if he's having an affair, in *sex, lies and videotape* (1989). Then she lays down in bed, still wearing the necklace. But moments later, it's gone.

Come Flub With Me

In the *Superman* parody which is part of *Hot Shots!* (1991)—itself a parody of *Top Gun*—watch as Charlie Sheen and Valeria Golino fly over the city. Her right earring, visible in the long shots, disappears in the close-ups. Since we're dealing with a parody within a parody from within the oh-so-warped mind of ZAZ's Jim Abrahams, is this a real flub or a parody of a flub—e.g., Yul Brynner's disappearing earring in *The King and I* (1956)? Your call.

So What Did She Use for Air?

In *Superman IV: The Quest for Peace* (1987), Nuclear Man (Mark Pillow) kidnaps Lacy Warfield (Mariel Hemingway) and takes her into outer space where she seems to have no trouble breathing—even without a space suit.

IN THE BALLPARK

There's no fan like a baseball fan. When studios start making movies about the national sport, they'd better watch their p's and q's and RBI's. The fanatic fans can spot any little glitch and it can drive them crazy. After all, when you're dealing with people who can quote stats back to Ty Cobb, do you think that they'd let a director get away with even the smallest baseball flub?

Flubdom seems to move from one filmic generation to another. *The Babe Ruth Story* (1948) was replete with historical errors. We are told that in his last game, Ruth hit three home runs and one single; actually he went hitless in one at-bat in that particular game.

Yet another from the film is that in the scene where Babe (William Bendix) hits his 60th home run in 1927 and rounds the bases, you can see signs on the Yankee Stadium bleachers for Ballentine Beer and Calvert Whiskey. Pretty daring for the park's owners, don't you think, since Prohibition was still in effect (until 1933)?

Then after seeing *The Babe* (1992), critic Gene Shalit went to the history books when, during the climactic game of the movie, a pinch-runner was used for a home run. Not in that particular game, Shalit says. Besides, another fan says, it's an error to use a pinch-runner on a home run.

Baseball films have been Hollywood favorites over the years. When they're flawed, fans are quick to take pen in hand. Some reports:

The First Shall Be Last

In *The Natural* (1984), Roy Hobbs (Robert Redford) is playing for the New York Knights, and the announcer makes it abundantly clear that the team's up in the bottom half of each inning. Hobbs wins the game with a home run; but he's on the visiting team and should be playing in the top of the inning. The home team always bats last.

Doubling the Error

Much has been made of Ray Liotta's right-handed batting portrayal of southpaw Shoeless Joe Jackson in *Field of Dreams* (1989). But an alert fan also noticed that while Shoeless Joe batted left, he pitched right-handed; just the opposite of the way Liotta plays the part. Also, Jackson—that he has his index finger outside his glove. That's a practice that didn't come into being until the fifties or sixties, not in Shoeless Joe's era.

A Series of Reverses

Eight Men Out (1988) had left-handed hitter Eddie Collins played as a right-hander, while Dickie Kerr, who threw left-handed, was seen pitching right-handed. In addition, the players in the picture are seen with a forefinger sticking out of their gloves. They wouldn't have in 1919, when the scandal took place.

Tricky Dickey

The Pride of the Yankees (1942) provided *FILM FLUBS* readers with a delightful tale about Gary Cooper's problems in batting left-handed and an editor's ingenious solution. Now there's more. In the film, Cooper, playing Lou Gehrig, looks in awe at the names of famous players on their lockers when he arrives in 1923. One of the names is Bill Dickey, later to become one of Gehrig's closest friends. But Dickey didn't join the Yankees until 1928. He also sees the names of Tony Lazzeri and Mark Koenig, both of whom joined the team after Gehrig.

We May Have to Revoke Their Dramatic License

Hard-core fans had a field day comparing on-screen events with reality in *The Pride of the Yankees* (1942). In one scene, Gary Cooper, as Lou Gehrig, tries to awaken his future wife (Teresa Wright) in the middle of the night by throwing pebbles at her window. A cop walks by and asks what he is doing there, and he says he's going to ask her to marry him.

Just prior to that scene, Gehrig and his teammates are seen beating the St. Louis Cardinals. Historians noted the Yankees beat the Cardinals only once prior to 1943—in 1928 when they swept the series. Gehrig and girlfriend Eleanor married in 1933, meaning that he strolled around for about five years on the way to her house.

In a touching scene, Babe Ruth (played by Babe himself) and Lou Gehrig promise a sick young boy that they will both hit homers for him, in a conversation in the boy's room in St. Louis. That would make it 1926 or 1928, the only years during Gehrig's career when the Yankees played World Series games in St. Louis. In the movie, Babe Ruth hits one home run and Gehrig hits two. There was no game in which this actually happened.

The real truth is that producer Sam Goldwyn moved the "called" home run of the 1932 Series from Chicago to St. Louis. The actual incident happened on October 1, 1932, and Ruth did hit two homers that day. Gehrig's two home runs in a World Series game against St. Louis were in 1928.

Ronnie Could Always Count on His Wife

Ronald Reagan seems to have always had wives, real or cinematic, who could stretch the truth, when convenient. Take *The Winning Team* (1952), for example, when he played pitcher Grover Cleveland Alexander. In his rookie year, which would make it 1911, Doris Day, playing Mrs. Alexander, is talking with the other players' wives before a spring training game. Referring to the opposing pitcher, she says "That's Eddie Plank. He won twenty games last year." In 1910, Eddie Plank won sixteen.

TIME WARPS

The Bible admonishes: "Let all things be done decently and in time,"[1] but movie making leans more toward Thomas Gray's description of Milton: "He passed the flaming bounds of place and time."[2]

Time warps—anachronisms—run rampant in the movies, involving set pieces, songs, props, even dialogue. Take a look at *Demetrius and the Gladiators* (1954), an epic set in A.D. 63, at the time of the Caesars, and recently rereleased on home video. Just behind and to the side of the royal throne in the arena scenes, you'll see Michelangelo's *David* among the heroic statuary. It looks great, but Michelangelo didn't sculpt it until about A.D. 1503, a mere 1,440 years later.

[1] I Corinthians, Ch. 14, V. 40
[2] *The Progress of Poesy*, V.2, 1.4

Long Time, No Funk

In a scene identified as "July 3, 1981," the young men in *Longtime Companion* (1990) dance to Sylvester's "Do You Want to Funk," a song that wasn't recorded until 1982.

The Christmas Conspiracy

We've uncovered some evidence that points to a conspiracy right within Oliver Stone's *JFK* (1991), evidence that could prove whatever we want it to prove (as some say the film did itself!). Seems that when Jim Garrison's fellow investigators are discussing Clay Shaw's use of the name "Clay Bertrand," they are sitting around Garrison's dining table, and there is a Christmas tree in the background. Garrison says he'll arrange a meeting with Shaw the following Sunday. That Sunday turns out to be Easter. Now…did he wait four months to set up the meeting with Shaw? Or did he create a clear and present danger in his own home by leaving a Christmas tree up for all that time, thus creating a fire hazard? Was it a "plant" (pun intended) to throw us off the trail? Perhaps we'll have to ask Oliver Stone to direct *Film Flubs: The Movie* to get the definitive answer.

Did It Take Him Four Years to Get Home?

A stamp collector noticed that in *Flying Leathernecks* (1951), coming home from the war, John Wayne takes a letter from a mailbox. In a full-screen shot, you can see a six-cent stamp—one that was issued in 1949, four years after the war ended.

A *Flub²* in Grease

Here's the kind of thing we love. A flub within a flub—or, you might say a flub to the second power. In *SON OF FILM FLUBS*, you were introduced to the mike boom, which is reflected in the shiny top of a jukebox as Olivia Newton-John plays it in the malt shop. Now a collector tells us that the jukebox itself is a reproduction model 1050, made in 1974, some twenty-five years after the setting of *Grease* (1978).

It Was a Long, Long Speech

Early in *The Rocky Horror Picture Show* (1975), the narration says that the action takes place on an early November evening. In the next scene, as Barry Bostwick and Susan Sarandon drive through the rain, Nixon's resignation speech plays on the car radio. Nixon resigned and gave that speech in August...in the daytime.

We Have It on the Highest Authority...

We have an admission of a film flub from no less than Disney's Jeffrey Katzenberg, who responded to a reader query in *Premiere*. Reader John E. Silva noticed that the money used in *The Rocketeer* (1991) was deutschemarks. But the film is set in the 1930s, when Germany's currency was the reichsmark (used from 1925 to 1948). Katzenberg acknowledged and apologized for the error in the magazine's Gaffe Squad column.

Come Rain or Come Time

In a World War II sequence of *For the Boys* (1991), Bette Midler sings "Come Rain or Come Shine." But the song wasn't written until after the war and wasn't introduced until 1946, when it was part of the musical *St. Louis Woman*.

Strings of Time

We owe this one to a guitar enthusiast who noticed that in *Places in the Heart* (1984), the picker in a scene set in the 1920s is using a C. F. Martin "Dreadnought"—a guitar not yet invented at that time—and on closer inspection found that the instrument was fitted with Grover Tuners, which weren't marketed until the early 1960s. Our same sharp-eyed spotter noticed that in *The Godfather, Part II* (1974), when young Vito (Robert De Niro) sits on the stoop with his wife and children, a man behind them is playing a Gibson-style guitar that wouldn't be invented for at least thirty years.

Bugged by Bugsy

A time glitch in *Bugsy* (1991) bugged not only Der Flubmeister, but almost everyone we know who saw the movie. Near the end of the film, after Bugsy's own house has been sold to finance the Flamingo Club, he takes another look at his "screen test." He's at Virginia Hill's mansion, but he looks at the film in the projection room of his old house. Huh?

They Didn't Stay Within the Lines

Once again, the colorizers weren't paying attention. When *It's a Wonderful Life* (1946) was given the treatment, those who wield the evil computer paintbrush colored in the family photographs around the house. They didn't realize that the film was set in an era when color photography was rare and not really available to the general public.

Judy and Larry and Perry

Richard Rodgers and Lorenz Hart come to Hollywood to score their first film in *Words and Music* (1948), laughingly referred to as their musical "biography." There, Judy Garland (as herself) joins Mickey Rooney (as Hart) singing "I Wish I Were in Love Again." Actually, the song was written not for a movie but for the 1937 Broadway musical, *Babes in Arms*, at which time Hart was about forty-two and Garland fifteen—they'd hardly have been show-biz buddies. And while we're on the subject of *Words and Music*, did anyone notice that Perry Como is cast as Eddie Anders, a fictional (?) buddy of Rodgers and Hart, and as Eddie sings a couple of their songs. However, at the all-star finale to the film, he is introduced as Perry Como to sing "With a Song in My Heart."

Far and Away Too Late

Today show film critic Gene Shalit points out in his review of *Far and Away* (1992) that Tom Cruise, Nicole Kidman, et al. arrive to join the Oklahoma Land Rush in 1892. Makes one wonder how they were able to stake a claim to any Oklahoma real estate, since the Land Rush took place three years earlier, in 1889.

An Inoculation to Keep the Beasts Away

Just as did Kirk Douglas in *Spartacus* (1960), Marc Singer follows suit in *The Beastmaster* (1982). Even though both movies are set in ancient times, both actors sport rather prominent vaccination scars.

Messing Around With Otis Redding

Otis Redding's songs are so popular that they're heard in all sorts of movies—and now and again, they slip time frames. In *Dirty Dancing* (1987), which takes place in 1963, you hear Redding's "Love Man," which wasn't released until after his death in 1967.

In *Top Gun* (1986), we hear that Tom Cruise's father was a fighter pilot who disappeared in 1965 or 1966. Yet in a later scene, Cruise tells Kelly McGillis that both of his parents loved "Sitting on the Dock of the Bay" by Otis Redding. The song was released in 1968.

Good Morning, World

A pivotal song in *Good Morning, Vietnam!* (1987) is "What a Wonderful World." The movie is set in 1965, but Louis Armstrong copyrighted the tune in 1967.

Welles Gets Wet

Orson Welles knew how to make a scene meaningful and moving, but he was all wet when in *Macbeth* (1948) he inserted one where King Duncan and his men renew their baptismal vows—led in a prayer composed by Pope Leo XIII in 1884. And think about this one: in *Marie Antoinette* (1938), viaticum is brought to the dying Louis XV (John Barrymore). The choir sings a Requiem Mass. Isn't that rushing things just a bit?

Grass Roots

Cher complains in *Mermaids* (1990) that Astroturf is going to ruin baseball. The movie takes place in 1963, and at the time artificial turf was still being developed under the trade name "Chemgrass." It wasn't until the carpeting of the Houston Astrodome in 1966 that the name "Astroturf" emerged.

Cape Fear

Cinema master Martin Scorsese is not immune from flubbing—even in a film as precisely and suspensefully assembled as *Cape Fear* (1991). Perhaps the most noticed flub in it happens when Ileanna Douglas and Robert De Niro chat in a bar. As she talks, the top button on her blouse is undone. Seconds later she buttons it, then it goes back to unbuttoned and buttoned without her ever touching it.

Later De Niro watches as Nick Nolte checks in at the airline ticket counter before boarding a plane. De Niro then asks the agent if Nolte is on the flight and when he is returning. Try that yourself and see what kind of response you get. According to a flub spotter in the know, airlines do not allow ticket agents to release this information. It takes a high-ranking official with proper security clearance to pull up a passenger list.

Young Juliette Lewis has a bit of a problem with the family vehicle. She says that she's grounded from driving the Jeep Cherokee as punishment for smoking. Unless somebody traded cars in the meanwhile, when the family flees they're in a Jeep Wagoneer. Small difference, but a goof nonetheless.

Another *Cape Fear* flub relates to Nick Nolte's statement that he had to go to hearings before the American Bar Association as a result of his criminal actions toward De Niro. We have this on high authority—no less than the Hon. Stanley M. Billingsley, of the 15th Judicial District of Kentucky. Judge Billingsley points out that the ABA doesn't license lawyers and has no authority to disbar them; it is a national lobbying association. Nolte would more properly have to go before the North Carolina Bar Association, given that Cape Fear is in that state.

MISMATCHES: THE MOTHER
OF ALL FLUBS

The classic of all film flubs is the mismatch—when things just don't add up from one shot to the next. Some things can get longer, shorter, or vacillate between the two, or there's a "mysterious healing" of broken glass, or disappearing bullet holes. There simply can be things that just don't make sense at all, or even change the meaning of the film. We offer:

Saving the Stunt

Mel Gibson handcuffs himself to a man he tries to trick out of suicide in *Lethal Weapon* (1987). The man jumps anyway, and as Mel falls with him, if you slo-mo the video, you'll notice that the rubber trick handcuffs break, so they join hands to complete the illusion.

Wilting Ardor

Michelle Pfieffer's mobster lover walks down the hall carrying a lavish bouquet of flowers in *Married to the Mob* (1988). When he arrives five seconds later, the bouquet has wilted to a skimpy business wrapped in white paper.

She'll Have Braids in an Hour or So

The baby in *Once Around* (1990) must have some amazing growth hormones. In the baptism scene, its hair grows from the time it is placed in Gena Rowland's arms to the time that Holly Hunter picks the child up and storms out of the room. We have to assume that this is because almost any scene involving an infant in a movie is filmed using twins or triplets. Screen Actors Guild and Child Welfare rules prohibit keeping a baby under the lights on a set for more than a very few minutes.

Hair of the Duke: The Adventure Continues

We're back on John Wayne's hair again. We told you about the problem with his hairpiece in *North to Alaska* (1960) in *FILM FLUBS*. Now we've learned that in *The Quiet Man* (1952) when he fights with Victor McLaglen, he isn't wearing his rug. So when McLaglen's first punch knocks Wayne's hat off, we see much less hair than he has anywhere else in the film.

A Reversal of Recollections

Again we have a report straight from the set...this time involving a scene in *Reversal of Fortune* (1990). Our reporter, who shall remain nameless for obvious reasons, saw a flub abornin' as a scene was being shot. But, on-set politics being what they are, he was in a lowly position where pointing it out could have been problematic, so he kept his mouth shut, and the gaffe went into continuity history.

Ron Silver and Annabella Scioria create contrasting flashbacks to compare Alan Dershowitz's theory with lady friend Sarah's. In her version, when Sunny von Bülow (Glenn Close) is dragged into the bathroom, a window is opened, providing evidence against husband Claus. While the Dershowitz version was being shot, someone forgot to open the window, actually changing the evidence and insinuating that he (Claus) did try to kill her. Our informant told the script supervisor about the error the next day and pointed out that the closed window was not part of the script, but was told it was too late to change it. So it's there on the screen, actually confusing the story. In fact, the bedroom window is also closed in one version, and von Bülow opens it in the differing version. So we're really confused by the whole business. You'll have to figure it out for yourself.

The Cagney Haymaker

James Cagney gives it to Robert Armstrong on the chin in *G-Men* (1935). But when Armstrong gets up from the floor, he has a black eye.

The Growing Bandage

After Kevin Kline cuts his finger while slicing a tomato in *Grand Canyon* (1991), his wife bandages it, covering about an inch of his finger. Then an earthquake hits, and they run outside. Barely a split second transpires, but the bandage now covers his entire finger.

Bogie Gets Familiar

Oh, no...we're on Bogie's case again. In *The Maltese Falcon* (1941), Sam Spade (Humphrey Bogart) is seated in a chair in front of Brigid (Mary Astor), who's sitting on a sofa. He leans forward to make a point—and in the next shot, he's on the sofa beside her.

131

Heston Changes Planes...and Changes Planes...and

An aviation buff noted that the use of so much leftover footage from *Thirty Seconds Over Tokyo* (1944), vintage Japanese war films, and stock War Department footage created aviation magic in *Midway* (1976). Charlton Heston, as Captain Matt Garth, takes off to bomb the last Japanese carrier in a Grumman TBM Avenger torpedo bomber, flies along with his men in a Douglas TBD Devastator torpedo bomber, attacks the carrier Hiryku with a Douglas SBD dive bomber, and then crashes to his death in a Curtiss SB2C Helldiver dive bomber (which didn't go into service until a year after the battle). The film also uses the Chance Vought F4UK Corsair and Grumman F6F Hellcat fighters, which weren't in use until well after the Battle of Midway.

More Notes on the Healing of Windshields

An automobile windshield is the subject of a quick healing in *Narrow Margin* (1990). Gene Hackman and Anne Archer are being chased by a sniper in a helicopter who shoots and breaks the windshield of their truck. But in the next shot, from the interior of the car, the windshield is just fine. Same thing happens in *The Godfather* (1972). When Sonny Corleone (James Caan) is ambushed by hit men, the very first shots completely shatter the windshield. He escapes, only to be riddled with bullets. After one of the hit men kicks him, there's a cut to shots which show the devastation on the toll station. Then there's a shot of the car on which we can see the bullet holes, but the windshield is still intact. And in *Cujo* (1983), when the dog attacks a mother and child, a broken windshield is suddenly restored.

Mismatches Making Mismatches

The action comedy, *The Hard Way* (1991), features Michael J. Fox and James Woods as a mismatched duo—but their roles are nothing compared to the mismatches which show up on screen. Early in the movie, the sweat stains on the neck of Fox's T-shirt continually go from larger to smaller to larger to smaller.

When the pair has a set-to in a movie theater, Woods starts the fight with his last two fingers taped together. When he throws Fox into a popcorn machine, there's no tape; in fact, he opens his hand wide. Then the tape is back again—on his index finger. And when Fox loses a shoe during the climactic fight atop the cigarette billboard, it sure seems that the shoe is back on again as he dangles from the sign and maybe even again when he's on an ambulance stretcher.

Joe Pesci—Best Supported Actor

Entertainment Weekly found that Joe Pesci had to face up to a flub in *My Cousin Vinny* (1992). To smooth a few years off the actor's face, makeup artists used "lifts"—tiny pieces of netting, glued to the skin, then pulled back under a toupee—said one of their number, Carmen Willis. But the devices tended to slip, slide, and disconnect, causing several scenes to be reshot. But the magazine reports that even so, some of the tabs can be seen in the finished film.

That'll Take the Curl Right Out of Your Hair

You can make your own joke about this one—but why, in *Final Analysis* (1992), was Kim Basinger's hair curly when she jumped into the sack with Richard Gere and, as a *Los Angeles Times* reviewer pointed out, "straight as an ironing board" afterward?

In and Out of the Dark

In *JFK* (1991), when in a restaurant with Kevin Costner, John Candy stands up from the table wearing his sunglasses. In the next shot, his hat is in his hand, but there are no sunglasses anywhere. Then when he puts the hat on his head, he's wearing shades again.

Similarly, in *Beverly Hills Cop II* (1987), Eddie Murphy as Alex Foley gets into a fight with a guard at a warehouse. Taking a punch, the guard's sunglasses fly off his face. After a few seconds of struggle with Murphy, he's wearing them again.

Engine Trouble

In *Always* (1989), when Holly Hunter bikes out to the airplane to say good-bye to Richard Dreyfuss, the right engine is shut down as she climbs up on the plane. Even though there was no opportunity to start it during the scene, when she climbs back down the engine's running.

Meet Me on the Porch Rail

Watch Judy Garland as she sits on a porch rail during the early part of *Meet Me in St. Louis* (1944). First she's sitting on the middle of the porch rail, then she's so close to the column that she can caress a rose, then she's back in the middle of the rail again.

Wet and Dry in Casablanca

Here we go—picking on *Casablanca* (1942) again. In a pouring rain, Rick (Humphrey Bogart) gets soaked while in a train station reading a note from Ilsa (Ingrid Bergman). In the next shot, when Sam hustles him onto the train, they're both perfectly dry.

Background Briefing

When William Petersen talks to his son in a grocery store in *Manhunter* (1986), they move down the aisles, then stop. Even though they're standing in the same place, carrying on the same conversation, somehow the background of canned goods changes as they talk.

LOOSE TONGUES

Actors spend a lot of time together on a set. Most shots take but a few minutes, then it's back to the trailer. There's time to chew the fat, play cards, even grab a "quickie" from time to time. They get to know each other rather well—not by their character names, but by their real names. Then when they're back on the set, sometimes they slip up and use the real name instead of the character name. And guess what? It gets into the final film, immortalized for us all to see and hear. Why? We can only assume that the editors were so wrapped up in their work, dealing with other problems, that they didn't notice.

Look and then listen for a few of our favorite "real names," as well as some other audio flubs:

No, Val, It's Jim They Want

Val Kilmer plays Jim Morrison in *The Doors* (1991). Near the end of the film, when he's in the shower with his girlfriend, the crowd is calling for him. She says, "It's you they want, Val."

An Improper Introduction

Tom Cruise plays race driver Cole Trickle in *Days of Thunder* (1990). When he meets Cary Elwes, as his rival Russ Wheeler, and Russ's wife as they walk alongside a lake, she greets him with "Hi, Tom."

The Case of the Subway Sex Change

USA Today film writer Susan Wloszczyna tells us that when she watched *Frankie and Johnny* (1991), she noticed that in a subway scene, a woman is on screen, but the voice we hear is that of a man. Hmmm...

Eat Your Heart Out, Milli Vanilli

When Michael Paré sings "On the Dark Side" in *Eddie and the Cruisers* (1983), he closes his mouth before his vocal solo ends.

An Impertinent Usher

Oh, no. We're back on the case of *Pretty Woman* (1990), winner of our first "Flubbie" for its plethora of gaffes. Now we find another: When Richard Gere and Julia Roberts are at the opera, the usher asks: "Will there be anything else, sir?" Gere says no, and the usher says, "the glasses are there, Julia." Julia's character was named Vivian.

A Ray of Sickness

In *Dead Again* (1991), Kenneth Branagh takes Emma Thompson to a restaurant, where he greets the owner as "Ray." Ray says that the place has no liquor license—and no music because Al, the piano player, is sick. A few minutes later, Branagh says: "What's going on? I can't believe it. No booze—and Ray's sick!"

137

A Well-Mannered Child

At the end of *Operation Petticoat* (1959), Cary Grant disembarks from the submarine and is met by Dina Merrill, along with a small boy and girl. The little boy says, "Hello, Mr. Grant."

The Writer Stands Accused

One has to wonder what kind of lawyer is defending Jodie Foster in *The Accused* (1988). When she is on the witness stand recalling her rape, he calls one of the men who raped her "the assaulter." Any law school graduate would have used "the assailant."

No, No, Douglas

Michael Douglas makes an emphatic point with Danny DeVito in *War of the Roses* (1989). As they look at house plans spread out on a desk, Douglas looks up and says, "No, no, DeVito!"

Lighten Up, Sly

When his pal Paulie (Burt Young) makes some disparaging comments about young boxer Tommy Gunn (Tommy Morrison) in *Rocky V* (1990), Rocky (Sylvester Stallone) responds, "Lighten up, Burt."

The Way We Almost Were

An editing cut near the end of *The Way We Were* (1973) has Robert Redford saying "ab awesome." Did an editor drop the "solutely"?

Little Man Tate

Believe me, it's tough to pick on the work of as fine an actress (and now director) as Jodie Foster, but when we hear the call, we must answer and charge on. Into the fray:

Early in her *Little Man Tate* (1991), notice that when young Adam Hann-Byrd displays his pianistic abilities to Dianne Wiest, he begins to play with his own short, stubby fingers. But when the shot cuts to hands on the keyboard, the fingers are now long and gracefully slim. Did Harry Connick, Jr., slip in and help the kid?

As the boy is introduced to his new chores while he stays with Wiest, he's suddenly wearing a Band-Aid on his head, the result of being hit with a globe tossed by Connick. The only problem is that the injury comes a few scenes *after* we first see the bandage. Unless the kid is unbelievably clumsy, the Band-Aid is on the exact spot where the globe hits him.

 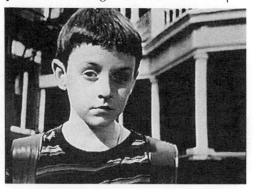

There's a prominent blunder right after the youngster stumbles in on Connick in bed with his girlfriend. When Connick talks to him outside the frat house, notice how the leather straps on the kid's backpack jump from shoulder to arm from shot to shot.

And finally, it appears that our Bruce Willis/Pacific Bell film flub (see *SON OF FILM FLUBS*) has spawned an offspring. Jodie Foster calls her son from a motel in Florida, where she is vacationing. But the area code on the phone isn't Florida. It's a bit difficult to decode on video, but one sharp-eyed viewer thinks it's "318," which would make it Louisiana; another opines that it's "315," even farther away in Oswego, New York.

TV TROUBLES

Searching out the goofs and screw-ups in television programs presents a real challenge. This is one arena wherein you have to be sharp of eye and quick of mind. It's fleeting flubdom. The gaffe you see flits away like a water sprite on electronic wings, and more often than not, unless you've taped the show, you don't have the opportunity to go back and take another look.

But our flub spotters are a bright and diligent lot. Some have an amazing talent, and we are pleased to report their findings:

Trekkin' Right Along...

In an interesting bit of cross-pollination from the TV series to the filmed version, in *Star Trek II: The Wrath of Khan* (1982), Ricardo Montalban (Khan) says he "never forgets a face" as he recognizes Walter Koenig (Chekov). Montalban is referring to the TV episode "Space Seed" in which he guested as Khan. However, Koenig was not a member of the cast when the "Space Seed" episode was filmed.

An Early Research Project

Obviously, there was some research going on back in the 1800s, according to evidence in *Son of the Morning Star*, a 1991 TV-movie about General George Custer. When he's hunting a herd of bison, one wears a red eartag.

Arrest the Sheriff

In an early episode of *The Andy Griffith Show*, Sheriff Taylor takes his girlfriend, Peggy McMillan (Joanna Moore), to a Raleigh restaurant for dinner. He orders a beer, and she has a mixed drink. The scene makes the pair into lawbreakers, since North Carolina didn't allow the sale of liquor by the drink at the time the episode was set, the early 1960s.

The Ears Have It

Eagle-eyed flub spotters just won't let a director get away with anything. Take, for instance, what happened in a TV movie, *Girl of the Limberlost* (1991). Several farmers noticed the heroine is picking seed corn during a storm. The ears she is picking and the stalks they come from are a lush green. However, she's actually picking roasting ears (corn on the cob). Seed corn is picked in the fall after the stalks and ears are dry and brown.

Alice Doesn't Ring There Anymore

Alice gets a telephone in the January 26, 1956, episode, "The Baby Sitter," of *The Honeymooners*. The number is BEnsonhurst 3-7741. However, between the original airing and the time the show went into syndication, it must have been discovered that it was someone's real number. In the syndicated version, even though you can see Jackie Gleason mouthing the original number, the number you hear is BEnsonhurst 3-5555.

Vinnie and Sonny...No Thelma and Louise

In the climactic episode of the famed six "arc" *Wiseguy* TV action-adventure, the setting is a movie house on New Jersey's south shore. The place is being locked up for the winter, as we see in the opening scene. Shortly thereafter, suave gangster Sonny Steelgrave (Ray Sharkey) manages to find his way in, figuring it's a good hideout from the feds who are pursuing him. Our hero, Vinnie Terranova (Ken Wahl), tracks him there and confronts him—over a bag of hot popcorn and a candy bar, before the two engage in fisticuffs, resulting in Sonny's electrocution when he is backed into some exposed wires. Our question is: if the place was closed for the season and locked up, why was the electricity left on, the popcorn machine poppin' away, and the concessions counter still packed with neatly displayed goodies?

Finding Time When You Need It

Calum (John McGlynn) tells James Herriot (Christopher Timothy) that he must rush to the train station in *All Creatures Great and Small* (1975), saying that he's going to pick up his girlfriend and doesn't have time to stand and talk with him. But he must have found time to change his shirt and tie, because they're different from what he was wearing a few moments before.

The Multi-Level Mohawk

Watch for varying heights of Mr. T's mohawk in episodes of *The A-Team*. Apparently his hairstylist didn't have a ruler.

Mladen...What a Fun Guy

Veteran actor Karl Malden, né Mladen Sekulovich, for years worked his own in-joke into whatever he was doing. On his *Streets of San Francisco* TV series, he invariably would take a moment during a dressing down of someone or other in his office to open the door and bark, "Get me a cup of coffee, Sekulovich!" to some unseen actor. And in one of his TV movies, *Word of Honor* (1981), while conversing with someone on the sidewalk, an extra walking by bumps him accidentally. Whereupon Malden, annoyed, yells after him, "Watch it, Sekulovich!"

Who Took the Jacket?

A jacket is hanging on a peg on the mirror when Tony Danza walks by in *Who's the Boss?* In the next shot, the jacket has mysteriously disappeared.

Weird Boston Weather

An episode of *Spenser: For Hire* has Robert Urich and his associate engaged in conversation, during which it is snowing in the close-ups, but not in the long shots.

The Confederate Faith Healer

Orry Main (Patrick Swayze) has a scar under one eye as he talks to President Jefferson Davis in *North and South, Part II*—but the scar heals and vanishes during the scene. Wonder if he had to make a "love offering" in Confederate dollars?

The Confederacy, Part II

In one of the old *Rin Tin Tin* episodes, two Civil War generals are having a sword fight on the steps of the courthouse. Suddenly two men in business suits walk out the door, look startled—as if someone told them to get off the set—and run out of the picture.

We're Talking Dead Drunk

An early 1990 episode of *L.A. Law* had Harry Hamlin representing a drunk driver. At one point, Hamlin said that the driver's breath test indicated an alcohol level of ".90." Later in the episode, it was corrected to ".09." Someone with a .90 level would either be dead or comatose. Our spotter wrote to *L.A. Law*, and the show 'fessed up to the error.

The Oddball Getaway

In the 1991 thriller, *Fever*, Armand Assante and Sam Neill are chasing all over town to get phone messages from the kidnapper of their mutual girlfriend. Ultimately they drive up to one phone booth in a single car, get the latest instructions, and then drive off in two separate cars. There was a car conveniently sitting there with the motor running! Later in the same film, Assante is temporarily stunned when taking a bullet just above the heart(!), then spends the remaining footage with blood dripping down his *right* arm.

An Early, Early Hank Williams Tune

The Virginian was set in the 1890s; but in an episode which introduces Randy Boone to the cast, he sings "I'm So Lonesome I Could Cry." Not bad. Hank Williams, who wrote the song, wasn't born until 1923.

Those Damned Specs

In the TV-movie, *Face of a Stranger* (1991), Gena Rowlands and Harris Yulin meet for lunch in a restaurant. In the first shot, over his shoulder looking at her, Yulin is seen adjusting his glasses to read the menu. In the opposite shot following, over her shoulder looking at him, he's just taking the glasses out of his inside coat pocket. The third shot, once again over his shoulder, finds him still fiddling with and adjusting his glasses that he is wearing.

Two Changes Make a Full House

In *Full House,* John Stamos's character name changed from Jesse Cochran to Jesse Katsapolous after the first season. Howcum? Did he change ethnicity also? In another show, little Stephanie (Jodie Sweetin) lost a baby tooth—but by the next show, it was back, full sized. Even though our reader wonders about this, we suspect that it was because most sitcom child parts are played by identical twins, to maintain a shooting schedule in compliance with child labor laws—and one had lost the tooth, the other hadn't.

Shannon's Mis-Deal

Elizabeth Peña plays a secretary, Lucy, in television's *Shannon's Deal,* but in a 1991 episode, twice Shannon (Jamey Sheridan) called her "Elizabeth"—once saying, "Will you come here, Elizabeth?"

What the 'L?

Supered over an establishing shot of a Nebraska town in *Lonesome Dove* (1989) is the name "Ogalalla." A later scene opens with a pan of a sign in the town, which now read, "Ogallala." The latter is the correct spelling.

The Diablo Made Me Do It

HBO's made-for-tv movie *El Diablo* (1990) is supposedly set in the Old West, yet in an aerial view, cars can be seen in the bottom of a valley.

A Yaletide Story

Our friend Bob Zeschin owns up to a flub in a Christmas movie he wrote—the wonderful *Story Lady* (1991), with Jessica Tandy. One of his characters is mentioned as having a MBA degree from Yale. Later, he found that Yale has no MBA program.

The Continuity Bombed Out, Also

An elderly couple plant a bomb in their car to blow it up as a protest in a *Starsky and Hutch* episode, but thieves steal the car, and our heroes must retrieve it before the bomb explodes.

A car buff noticed that when the car is stolen, it's a 1963 Chevy Impala two-door hardtop. When the thieves remove the masking paper after repainting it, it's a 1964 Impala two-door sedan. When the police dispatcher reports it stolen, he calls it a 1973 Chevy. Then, when the car finally explodes, it's a 1963 Chevy Bel Air two-door sedan.

Mugato...Gumato...Either Way, It's a Mean Sucker

In the *Star Trek* episode "A Private Little War," a creature on the planet Neural is called a "Mugato" by Captain Kirk, one ever-diligent flub spotter noticed. Later, Nona (Nancy Kovack) calls the same creature a "Gumato." Either way, it's a mean sucker, our spotter reports.

ENDNOTE

The quality of our flub spotters is no less than amazing. In this book, you'll find flubs contributed by producers, directors, actors, film school students and teachers, a judge, a magazine editor, film writers for various newspapers and magazines, television commentators, our publisher, even the Prior of an order of Jesuits. We've had a script supervisor point out flaws in her own work—an actor tell us to watch as he flubs on-screen—a production assistant relate how he spotted a gaffe as it was being shot, but couldn't persuade the director to reshoot. Perhaps the founding of a blue-ribbon flub spotter squad, an advisory board if you will, is in order.

We've received literally thousands of letters, and since this is essentially a one-person operation (we're flattered by the number of people who wrote to "the Film Flubs organization"), we hope the lack of a timely response doesn't connote any lack of appreciation for your making the effort to share your favorite flubs. The task is daunting, but we're chipping away at it.

Whenever we're tired or in a sinking mood, all we have to do is open your letters, read the nice things you have to say about the *FILM FLUBS* books, enjoy and quite often have a good laugh at the information you've imparted about your flubs.

Believe it or not, we also appreciate the letters pointing out some of the glitches that crept into the previous books. A couple were due to the rush to meet a publication deadline and were corrected in later printings; a few were based on differing interpretations of the same information; and one or two have no explanation at all. But perhaps they're proof of the pudding: just as film gaffes slip right past an array of department heads, script supervisors, editors, and even directors, so they slip right through the book editing process and onto the printed page.

In *FILM FLUBS*, our most egregious error was the confusing of novelist D. H. Lawrence (*Lady Chatterly's Lover*) with T. E. Lawrence (*Seven Pillars of Wisdom*)—although even the *New York Times* did it in a piece on the 1960s Terence Rattigan play, *Ross*, which was about Lawrence of Arabia (T. E., that is). We knew better, but it slid off our fingers right onto the keyboard, into the computer, and onto the printed page. Another was our identifying the *Lusitania* as a German luxury liner; it was British. And we charged a "bouncing wall" error to *Jewel of the Nile*; again, it was a slip of the microchip, since the flub belonged to its sister film, *Romancing the Stone*. And since we were a bit merciless in pointing out "flipped film" errors, the gremlins had their moment with our picture of *North by Northwest*; it was printed backwards.

The gremlins caught us again in *SON OF FILM FLUBS*. We well knew that it was Celeste Holm carrying the baby in our *Three Men and a Baby* item—but as literally hundreds of letters pointed out, we misidentified her as Olympia Dukakis. Why? Who knows? And why did it pass all the checks and balances? Just like film gaffes do.

Likewise, we have to acknowledge our error re Teri Garr in the *Close Encounters of the Third Kind* item. It was, of course, Melinda Dillon. And yes, we knew that the bookcase in *Back to the Future* was in Doc's house. Why we said it was at the school gym, who knows?

Enough confession. Our soul is cleansed. We shall go and try to sin no more.

Back to business: we're really flattered that so many readers are anxious to see their names immortalized in the flub spotter squad. With each addition, the number grows to the point that the type must get smaller and smaller to accommodate the names without taking over half of the book. Such is again the case with this edition.

Also, many of the flubs discussed herein were reported by a number of readers. Sometimes, the name listed is the first contributor; others either described it best or contributed some useful information. In other cases, it's sort of a "name lottery." As an example, some of the same flubs in *Terminator 2: Judgment Day* were noticed by fifteen or twenty readers. Likewise those in *Robin Hood: Prince of Thieves* and many other films. We really couldn't list them all.

But please keep writing; perhaps we can include yours and your name in a future edition. You may well be the only person who notices a particular flub.

If you want the series to continue, or to let us know about the flubs you've spotted, please write:

FILM FLUBS
P.O. Box 551
Hollywood, California 90046

Again, sincerest thanks. It gives us great joy to know that these books have brought such pleasure to so many people.

Bill Givens
May 1992

THE SHARP-EYED, QUICK-WITTED FILM FLUBS SPOTTER SQUAD

Keith Adams, Mary Ann Ahern, Christopher Alford, Amoretta Allison, Melissa Anderson, Shawn M. Anderson, Richard Van Arman, J. Douglas Arnold, Christa E. Arvantes, Jim Atkins, Marie Aucone, Jerry Azzaro, Bill Baker, Stan Baldwin, Dr. Howard Bargman, Amy Barnes, Amy Bass, Judith Batten, Ky Beard, Henry Cabot Beck, Mitch Beck, Suzanne Wells Bergman, Jerry Berkowitz, Dale Berryhill, Scott Biggers, Terie Biggs-Greenan, Judge Stanley M. Billingsley, Nancy Blevins, Joel Bloom, Dan Bollinger, Damien Bonito, Hal Bornkamp, Julie Klein Boshwit, Kelly Boutin, Christopher A. Brame, Diane Branston, Jason Brown, Sean Bury, Dana Bushman, David W. Campbell, Larry Candela, Ron Carlson, Pauli Carnes, Sharon A. Carrish, Danielle Carter, Don Casalone, John Cassidy, Darin Chambers, Aaron Chauncey, Kenny Chesier, Sean-Francis Chew, Dean Chu, Terrie Clark, Arthur C. Clarke, Adelaide Leigh Cleare, Phillip Cleveland, Cherie Clineff, James Clink, Adele Cohen, Mort Cohen, Steven B. Cohen, Leah Cohosskubins, Tom Condo, Bonnie Cooper, Michael Crichton, Jay Crosby, Ann Culligan, Steve Daly, Ellis W. Darby, Rita Davison, Stanley Donen, Greg Donio, Rich Drees, Andy Durstin, John Eby, Debbie Erlich, Fr. Wlliam J. Federer, Lance S. Fisher, Chuck Flagg, Gregory Fox, Mark Frazier, Andrew Friedenthal, Martin Friedenthal, Keith M. Gallagher, Pat Galloway, Vance Garnett, Bob Gaskin, Carrie Gasparic, Steven Geller, Mark H. Gerner, Debbie Gilbert, Karen Gilley, Rob Givens, Avrum and Joanne Glassoff, Paul D. Glicker,

Ellis Godard, Mary Lynn Gottfried, Brian Graff, Howard Grant, Tina Gustafson, Monica Hammerschmidt, John S. Harris, Jay Hartman, Dixon Hayes, Martha Heneger, David Hinckley, David and Carrie Hiser, Cheryl Hodges, Willie Holmes, Candee Hopkins, Greg Hotchkiss, Lori Hull, Mark Hunt, Alan Hurley, Peggy Hwang, William C. King III, Donald G. Ingraham, Robert Ingram, Hope Ismailorski, J. C. Jewell, Suzanne Johnston, Ian Jones, Eric Kabakoff, Stephen Kaufman, James Kerwin, Gregory Kirchling, Nevella L. Kiter, Kacy Koch, Carol Koomey, Christopher Kush, Dave Lachance, Bryon Laird, Jo Larzelere, Debbie Leatham, Ian W. Lebby, Danny Lerner, Adam Levenberg, Richard Louie, Dr. David J. Lubin, Brian M. Lucas, Kimberly Lucas, Sharon Lunder, Tim T. Lyman, Sarah-Kate Lynch, Michelle Macaluso, Jason Majik, Nicholas J. Maksymyk, Leonard Maltin, Al Marill, Phil Marsh, Kenneth Martz, Craig T. Mason, Brent Maxey, Brian McCormick, Jeff McGinnis, Heidi McKelrath, Shawn McLaughlin, Rob Medich, Belden Menkus, David Merliss, Corey Mesler, Bill Method, Jerry Meyer, Paula Meyers, Janie Miller, Shawna Mioduski, Tera Jean Molchan, Tracy A. Moore, Ruth Moss, Bill Moushéy, Linda Murray, J. Allen Nelson, Alex Newborn, Billy Norris, John Odre, Robert Osborne, John Ostendorf, David Parker, Todd Parker, Kent Parks, Cheryl Patterson, John Patterson, Ben Petrone, Mark Petty, Craig Phillips, Jason Prather, Casey Preece, Kristin Price, Allan Provost, William J. Purpura, Christina Radish, Robert Ralston, Anna and Alan Rast, Clete Reid, Kim Reilly, Mike Reynolds, Christian de Rezendes, Tim Rice, Sean Roberts, Patrick Robertson, Aaron Robinson, Joan Romick, Thomas Rosales, Paul Rosen, Barbara L. Ruehl, Kim and David Rumball, John J. Russo, Colin Ryono, Josh Sabarra, Tim Sacco, Zed Saeed, Robin Sagan, Diane Sanders,

Wllliam G. Sanders, Chris Schaffren, Sean Schindler, Peter and Adrien Schouten, Erkia Schwartz, Baker Scott, Brian Scott, Kyle Setzer, Gene Shalit, Jack Sharkey, Bill Shoemaker, William Shoudis, Eric Shuler, Peter Silveri, John E. Silvia, Robert and Kathy Sizemore, Margaret Sloane, Brian D. Smith, Drew Smith, Ken Spitzer, C. G. Stern, Brian Stone, Charles E. Stramiello, Dave Strauss, Todd C. Sullivan, Bernard J. Sussman, Sharon Sussman, Fred Swan, Jeff Swanson, Kurt and Priscilla Taube, Mark Taylor, Joel Thomas, Helen Thompson, Jusin Thorpe, Andrea J. Tice, Betty Tiska, Veronica Trybalski, William J. Trzeciak, Jeff Valentine, Jim Verburg, Cliff Watkins, Lindell Webb, Mary Wehrheim, Liam Wescott, Jeffery L. White, Todd Whitford, Bill Whitney, Brendan Wilhelm, Norman Wilner, Pam Wilt, Shonn Wiscarson, Susan Wloszczyna, Henry Wong, Janet Zak, Tracy Zak, Bob Zeschin, Kathryn Zigmont, Marco and Beth Zirogiannis, Bill Zuk, Armanda Zukar

TITLE INDEX